WATER, THANK GOD!

BY

DICK A. RICHARDS

As much as possible the editor has left the author's original words, phrases and arrangement intact throughout the book.

Edited by
Ethel R. Branson

Sketches by
Dick A. Richards
and
Connie Asch

ISBN 0-918080-14-2

TREASURE CHEST PUBLICATIONS, INC.
1842 W. Grant Road * Suite 107
P. O. Box 5250
Tucson, Arizona 85703

DICK A. RICHARDS

FOREWORD:

"ALL THINGS BRIGHT AND BEAUTIFUL, ALL
CREATURES GREAT AND SMALL,
ALL THINGS WISE AND WONDERFUL THE
LORD GOD MADE THEM ALL.
HE GAVE US EYES TO SEE THEM AND LIPS
THAT WE MIGHT TELL,
HOW GREAT IS GOD ALMIGHTY WHO HAD
MADE ALL THINGS WELL."

---Cecil Frances Alexander

In every minute detail, each of all living things encompassed in the above words, being elements of nature in the beginning, needed water to survive, progress and blossom to capacity according to natural life. It is rarely that those, who have had a life-time of experiences in natural husbandry, are able and willing to communicate to others the conclusions they have reached through so much effort. The incessant round of duties on the farm and with nature, and the frequent development of new problems prove too absorbing of time and energies. There is, however, no doubt that, to the writer, the task of reviewing his experiences clarifies his aims and equips him for further investigation.

To the reader already engaged in the initial stages of the primary area of water dowsing, there is much to be gained from reading an account such as Dick A. Richards has written. It is a development of the neighborly practice of "peering over the hedge" by which the most capable and successful dowsers of all ages have been able to extend the limits of their own experiences.

To the beginners in water dowsing and the forked branch a writing such as this affords an

3

opportunity for gaining an insight into dowsing practices and the philosophy of underground water, which would otherwise be impossible.

Many readers will note that the conclusions reached by Mr. Richards, may differ from widely accepted theories. Water dowsing, though as old as the ages and commonly practiced today in the Old World, is a newly developed and slowly accepted practice here in the United States of America. I would be rendering a disservice, to the spirit of dowsing research, to assume that the last word has been written on many of the subjects that are put forward in these writings. Unlike the experiments conducted in a laboratory, which can be brought within the same narrow limits of variation, whether conducted in New York, London or Moscow, each situation of the dowser may offer peculiar conditions requiring individual study. Development of the critical faculty is an important preparation for dowsing and no doubt for other walks of life. Mr. Richards' shrewd and seasoned observations are stimulating in this respect.

LUCAS D. PHILLIPS

Attorney, Judge,
Virginia Legislator Assembly
Leesburg, Virginia

THIS WRITING IS DEDICATED TO:

First, MY DEAR WIFE OF FORTY THREE YEARS
OF MARRIAGE,
for her understanding and putting up with me.

Second, LUCAS D. PHILLIPS, For his
encouragement and friendship.

Third, ALL THE TOM HATCHERS, for their
kindness and warmth.

Fourth, TO ALL DOWSERS EVERYWHERE.

"LANG MAY YER'R LUM REEK"

DICK A. RICHARDS

THE REASON WHY

Not many writers can claim to have a private coach to keep them on the job, but I can boast of one. My friend, Lucas D. Phillips, has always encouraged me to keep on with dowsing over almost 20 years. It is with great pleasure that I convey my gratitude to him for his kindness, advice and help.

My grateful thanks go to Tom Hatcher for his belief in me and to Kenneth Roberts and his book "Henry Gross and His Dowsing Rod" from which I gained much. Also to Harvey Howells and his book "Dowsing For Everyone," with it's commonsense insight. Most important is the encouragement, always, from my wife, her understanding and love being an asset beyond any worldly price.

Finally, with sincere respect to the elements of underground water, the power between the forked branch, natures law and the human, the reason why such action exists, I know not.

Dick A. Richards

PREFACE

This account is the true experiences of Dick A. Richards as a water dowser. He tells of how he first became a dowser. His many interesting and educational experiences finding water for technicians, bureaucrats, and home owners were sometimes quite humorous.

This is an interesting and intriguing example of how a man can become an accomplished and professional dowser and he can and does find water and he finds it in some very unlikely places.

This account contains numerous lessons in dowsing and a valuable treasury of useful hints and suggestions in practical dowsing.

Anyone, even an experienced dowser can learn from another dowser and much can be learned from these experiences of Dick A. Richards.

He gives outstanding proof that DOWSING DOES WORK.

Oscar T. Branson

"There is a place, a need for books like "WATER, THANK GOD!", which I've just read with pleasure—an honest account, by an honest man, with a feel for what is going on, and the experience to back up his story."

Terry Ross

CONTENTS

CHAPTER 1

THE BEGINNING OF IT ALL

The following is a rough account of my experiences with the dowsing rod, and with people, circumstances and attitudes over the past almost twenty years, which I hope may advance and help in the location of underground water for those who are in need of water. Also to encourage the skeptic to see that this is not witchcraft or a game to play, but a God-given gift, which is probably in all of us, waiting to be exercised and developed in a serious manner and not to be ridiculed or made light of.

I don't know how it works, but I do know of it's enormous power and I have seen the effect of this on different individuals. I have learned, as I practiced and saw the results, to respect such power and know without any hesitation the DOWSING ROD DOES WORK.

Who and what am I? I was born in 1913 in County Durham, in the North of England. My father was Welsh and my mother was Scottish. I took a ship for Canada in February 1928 at the age of fifteen years. I logged in the winter, farmed in the summer, did some trapping, hunting, fishing, riding, etc, and have been with nature mostly. I was three and one half years with a cavalry regiment, and five and a half years in the R.A.F., Second World War. I studied agriculture in my spare time. After the War, I became a farm and property manager. I came to the U.S.A. in 1952, under contract as a farm manager. I studied at Cornell University, wrote a few articles for the Hereford Journal and finally settled here in Loudoun County, Virginia. I am a past member of the Izac-Walton League, a ten year board member of the Leesburg Architectural Review Board, a Realtor Associate, a court appointed member of the Loudoun County Equalization Taxation Board, a Commissioner of the County Arbitration Board, a past member of the Real Estate Grievance Committee and, very fortunately, I am a WATER DOWSER. Oh I forgot, also, I am a Senior Citizen!

It was back in 1929 in Ontario, Canada; my employer at that time was Mr. John Varty. He was a wonderful man and at 70 years of age could vault up onto a bare-back horse and could hit a dime with a Winchester rifle at 30 yards. We were running some fence lines through a swamp and on the way home in the evening he said, "Dick have you ever tried this?" and proceeded to open his stock knife. He went to a willow tree and cut a low hanging branch. He stripped off all the leaves and cut the ends off the branch, leaving himself a forked or Y branch about two feet long, like this:

He then held the ends of the fork in his hands with the palms facing upward and the leg of the fork facing out in front of him, pointed up at about a 45 degree angle. We were walking along a lane between the stone walls and as he walked slowly along, the end of the forked stick would bob down and up. At one point as it began to go down, he stopped and the leg of the forked stick pointed over and down at about 45 degrees and I remember his face showing that he was using strength to hold the ends of the branch.

Well, as a boy in the North of England, I had heard of "Water-Witches" and "Diviners" and had no reason to question what I saw now, because in Europe it was common knowledge that water could be found in this manner. John Varty then had me go back about 20 feet up the lane, had me hold my hands out, palms up, and he placed the ends of the forked branch across my palms and under my thumbs.

He told me to grip the ends, keeping the point upward. He then had me walk slowly toward a stone he had left as a marker in the lane at the spot where the stick went down for him. It seems like yesterday, but that was about 50 years ago. As I came within four or five feet from the stone, the stick began to move downward, which made me grip harder. As I got within a couple of feet from his marker, I could no longer hold against the downward pull of the stick. I relaxed and turned to John whose face was all smiles at my astonishment.

I don't remember our exact conversation as we proceeded on home, but I do recall his telling about his parents and boyhood out in Medicine Hat and how he had been shown how to hold the forked stick by older members of his family. I was intrigued and played with forked sticks several times after that but gradually forgot about it.

About 30 years and many experiences later, a gentleman, Lucas D. Phillips, gave me a book to read, "Henry Gross and His Dowsing Rod," by Kenneth Roberts. That was when my dowsing education began. Mr. Phillips is a true "Virginia Gentleman". It is an ever increasing honor to call him my friend. He is a great public servant of the State of Virginia and Loudoun County. Lucas Phillips, Col. Mason (a prominent county resident) and Tom Hatcher (Hatcher's Plumbing) got in touch with Henry Gross, who came and dowsed for water locations. Lucas needed a well for a new house and also a commercial well in the east end of town. Col. Mason needed water for his estate and Tom Hatcher was interested in water for the town.

Lucas Phillips lives just west of Leesburg on a hilltop called Fort Johnston, an advantage point used by the Confederates in the Civil War. The rifle and observation abutments are still there. Three states, Virginia, West Virginia and Maryland, can be seen from this point as well as several counties, The Blue Ridge Mts., Bull Run Mts., The Short Hill and the Catoctin Range. On a clear day, with binoculars, the Washington Monument can be seen about thirty miles away. It is magnificent country, with the Potomac

River flowing away to the east. Lucas got a good supply of clean water at about 300 feet. While Henry Gross was up there, he held his dowsing rod out over the countryside and at one point facing north, out toward the Catoctin Range, he said, "Eight miles out there in that range, there is a big dome of water rising." Henry marked a site in the east end of town which, when drilled to about 250 feet, brought in 300 gallons per minute and the depth could not be lowered with the pump they used. Col. Mason had a site marked by Henry and, at 100 feet, vast quantities of water came forth and Henry is reported to have said that there was a great body of water flowing under the area.

At the Paxton Home For Boys at the north end of town, there is a mighty flow of water from a big well and there are caverns underneath. Tom Hatcher told me he had been lowered down into the well in a sling and he had a five foot piece of 2 x 4 lumber with him and a light. His light beamed on the body of water below him and he dropped the length of wood into the water. It turned round and round a couple of times then disappeared into the caverns.

I relate the above to show that on the top of a mountain or at sea level, it made no difference to Henry Gross and it would seem that great bodies of water flow within the earth. This would appear to be proven by Henry Gross finding water domes in Bermuda where previously only brackish water had been found. The populace depended on rain water off the roofs, and tanker ships bringing water in. With the sea all around, the domes of clear good water found by Henry must have come from the earth below sea level.

It has been my experience that there are veins of good water 25 to 50 feet down in loam or shale, but wells have been drilled to 500 and 600 feet, through solid rock, and have gone into cavernous areas where enormous quantities of water are flowing. My experiences are as nothing compared to Henry Gross'. He was an amazing human being who had developed a talent, not through any scientific knowledge or academic degree, but through basic common sense and much practice. He must also have had a sincere respect for the power of the laws of nature and knew that one must work with nature and not against her. I never expect to become anywhere as proficient as Henry Gross, but I believe I can show in the following pages, even though I don't know how, that the dowsing rod works wonders and can work for many people. All of my life I have known that nothing in nature is equal, but always perfectly balanced. Yet it is generally the attitude of humans to try to make everything equal and in so doing cause imbalance.

I never kept detailed records on every individual well site I found for people, but I guess the total sites would be about 200 here in Loudoun County and surrounding areas, with about 6 failures (causes unknown).

I will first try to explain how I proceed, what I feel, how I obtain place, depth and gallonage and, as I recall, some of the circumstances, the people and the attitudes. I learned a lot from Kenneth Robert's book about Henry Gross and found that, with practice, more knowledge came to me in ways that were unexpected and surprising. So I recommend to all would-be dowsers, read about Henry and his rod, his simple comments and reasons, his honest opinions and his manner of practice.

It seems that no two dowsers operate exactly the same, though the end result is never in doubt. I have been asked on occasion to survey a given area, where, unknown to me, a previous dowser has been employed and his facts noted. After I had completed my scanning and given my opinion, the owners compared both sets of figures and the location and found they matched amazingly, but said we did it all in a different manner, but came to the same conclusion.

One case in particular had to do with geologist, Les King, who was the head of the County Conservation Department. He came to me some years ago and asked me to go with him to a 100 acre tract of land that was being considered for an animal shelter. Four wells had been drilled along a ridge to about 400 feet deep, at $6.00 per foot, (four dry dust holes). So I went, and Les and the future shelter manager followed me around most of one afternoon and took notes. Finally I had marked four sites with pegs and as I finished, Les King said, "Dick, we have been pulling a fast one on you all day. Some days ago we had geologists here and the four sites you indicate are not 12 inches away from each of their sites.

CHAPTER 2

THE FORKED STICK WORKS

Finding that the forked stick worked for me, my good friend Lucas D. Phillips, encouraged me to experiment more with it. On many occasions we traveled about together, walking many miles here and there. Even when in a car with him, I would hold the dowsing branch out in front of me and it would move up and down as we went along the country roads. I have used cherry, peach, willow, elm and maple branches and have no special reason for it, but I like young maple best and I began to learn how to detect where an underground vein was located. I began by scanning an area, using the 360 degrees of a circle first. I would hold up the rod and turn first to my right, then to my left and see if I could feel any movement. I found that if there was a feeling to the far right there generally was one also to the left. I then turned 180 degrees, or half the full circle, in one direction. Then I would face completely around in the opposite direction and pace 4 or 5 paces into the other half of the 360 degrees and do the same right to left scanning. If I got the same feeling at each end of the swing around, I knew there must be an indication of a central area behind me, or somewhere midway between the two 180 degree halves, as shown here.

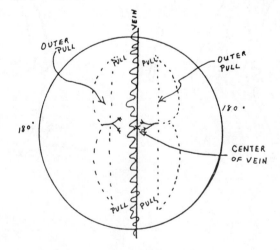

I would then walk to the outer edge of my imaginary circle, at right angles to the position where I started, and holding up the rod, walk slowly toward the center. At the first indication of the rod going down I would stop. This gave me the feeliing of the outer edge of the pull and I found that as I reset the rod up again it would stay still, until I began to move forward again. Then it would begin to move downward and get stronger until it pointed straight down and I could no longer stop or hold it. I would mark both of these places, at the first indication or the outer edge, then at the center. I would then repeat this procedure from the opposite side of the circle and I found the distance between each outside edge and the center were exactly the same, like the radii of a circle, sometimes greater, sometimes smaller, depending on the size of the circle. To me this indicated the width of the stream's vibrations or emanations (I still do not know what or which). However this gave me a central spot and it was no problem then to find the direction the vein flowed and it's underground path could be followed and mapped.

Now, to find depth, I would stand over the center of the vein and walk away from it at right angles. When I could no longer hold the rod up, I would stop, let's say at 40 paces. This indicates 120 feet down. Holding the rod up again, it would stay still until I moved forward and then it would move and finally go down again, perhaps at 3 paces, or 9 feet, an indication to me of 9 gallons per minute (Bishop's Rule).

Then to know how high the water would rise in the casing after the well was drilled, I would stand over the center again and pace backwards and, at say, 8 paces this would signify that water would rise to within 24 feet of ground level. So if one had a 224 foot deep well, there would be 200 feet of water in a 6" casing and at 1 1/2 gallons per foot this would give a reservoir of 300 gallons of water. This is always good to know before you seal in a submersible pump. All of this certainly took time, as practice was not continuous, but only on occasion.

Often I would ask Lucas, why does it do this or why should that happen and he would say the reason that this happened was because of what previously happened, or was about to happen.

My pacing-off across the land to find depth, is like Henry Gross said, "What do you do if you are on the edge of a cliff?" So he found ways around such difficulties, which I am now finding, by using two wire rods (explanation later). So one is always learning and it becomes more mysterious and it takes so long to see and know the enormous power within nature. Therefore one can see why only the older, or old, have gained enough knowledge to be able to have a deep seated respect for the unlimited powers of nature and they alone are able to hand down practices to others only after they themselves are advanced in age.

It is very peculiar how the dowsing rod can sap my strength. About 10 or 15 minutes after I begin to use the rod, I get an ache at each side of my neck. The cords feel tight and I feel a slight exhaustion, but if I stop for a few minutes and rest, I can go on with no problem. Sometimes people around me will say "Are you alright Dick?" as they evidently see some slight distress. Of course I tell them it's O.K., it is just the initial feeling of the rod. There is no point in going into a long explanation of the actual feeling in my neck. They would no doubt think I was putting on a show.

Miss Evelyn Penrose, a British dowser, who was employed by the British Government in Africa and British Columbia, was mentioned in Kenneth Roberts' book on Henry Gross. Miss Penrose stated that she felt exhausted at times as though some inner strength was taken from her body and after much use of the rod her hands were blistered and calloused. She said there were times when she was dowsing large quantities of oil or minerals and she was seized with violent physical sickness. This, to me, points to the fact that we have not even begun to understand the slightest rays, vibrations or different chemical examinations that come from Mother Earth and surround us. It may even prove to be a completely new discovery of natural power, with unbelievable assets to mankind, but this is away out of my realm. I wish I had been able, financially, to take the time many years ago to study and practice much, much more. My progress has been slow due to very limited time. However I am now able to walk onto a tract of land and, knowing where a well is required for a residence or other building, I can very quickly know, through a circular scan, where the nearest water is located. As I circle, I can tell by different pulls, that there is water at considerable distance away.

I am dumbfounded when I am called to find a well site on a 5 acre tract where the residence is completed, the lawns laid and the landscaping completed and the owner says he must have a well in a particular area, 6 feet from the back of the house and near the kitchen. It has to be here in this specific spot, because the septic tank and field are on the other side of the house and the health department says this is where the well should go. I explain to him that water is where it is, not where you want it, or where you think it should be. He should have established his well site in the beginning before he began to build. He soon saw the point and looked somewhat sheepish. Then he said, "I hope you can help me and find a site close to the spot I have just indicated". They just don't understand!

I had a call from a chap who had built a fine home, probably about $120,000.00, on a 3 acre tract. He said a builder friend had told him to call me before he built his house and get me to find a site for him. But his father-in-law had said, "Go ahead and build, there's plenty of water around here". So he went ahead and built. They drilled 3 sites, to an average depth of 250 feet and picked up about a half gallon per minute, at a cost of $4,000 to $5,000. Then he asked if I would come and see if I could help. I went and found two places for him to drill. They now have enough water, but he had learned the hard way.

Then one gets the smart alec who says, "I suppose now that you have marked this spot, all I have to do is stick a pipe in the ground and fasten a spigot to it and just turn on the water". Generally it is very satisfying when you leave, and later when you hear, that your predictions were correct and another family with a farm and livestock have plenty of water.

Very often one hears of final results in round about ways. Most people call me and tell me what happened and how the actual results compared to my predictions; but others are very peculiar. They want you to come immediately and want to know where to get hold of you when they are in need. But once they have their water, they have lost your address and forgotten all about you!

The requirement here in Virginia is 100 gallons of water per day per person and where there is a four bedroom house to be built, a minimum 800 gallon septic tank is required. Additional bedrooms require a bigger tank, as they estimate that 2 people occupy each bedroom. Other additions, as bathrooms etc., do not affect the septic system. It is when you add an extra bedroom that you affect the septic system because of additional people. Generally a flow of 3 gallons per minute, or 180 gallons per hour, or 3,320 gallons per day would be ample for a small village. So it can be seen that 2 gallons per minute is enough for a family of 8 people in a four bedroom house.

Naturally everyone likes to have abundant water from their wells. To help this situation, it would be best to ascertain if there is enough water at the location of any proposed house site. We have areas here of rock that are several hundred feet deep, but close to the surface there are only small pockets of water. Generally, once a drill is through such rock, there is an abundant supply of water.

Everywhere I am asked to go to locate a well site, there are those who are interested enough to ask how the rod works. I try to show them how to hold the rod to see if they can get any reaction. I would say about 50% do get the feeling of the rod moving for them. I take great pleasure in seeing the amazement of those who were skeptics or outright unbelievers, when the rod moved strongly for them.

Tom Hatcher, the senior owner of "Hatcher's Plumbing", has called upon me many times to locate water for new houses or old homes where springs have gone dry. In one instance an old well within an old colonial house had been turned down as "unfit" by the health department and a new site had to be found. Tom drove me to the property, which was high up in the Catoctin Range. The land was about 3 acres, but due to it's shape and the position of the septic field, there was only one location, of about half an acre, which could be utilized for a well site. Very luckily for the owners, I found a spot and, I remember, I got 5 gallons per minute at 250 feet. As I finished and Tom drove a stake in at the spot, the owner's two children, a boy and a girl of about 7 to 8 years old, who had been watching, came over to me and the little boy asked me, "May I try that please?" I said, "Sure you can", and I began to place the rod in his hands. The mother came running out and pulled her boy away and told me she did not want her children to touch the forked stick and I was not to allow them to touch it. I explained to her there was no harm at all in the rod and that she herself should try it and see, it might work for her too. But she threw up her hands and said, "Don't come near me with that", and fled to the house. Tom told me afterwards that the family was from France and the lady had severe reservations about the dowsing rod. He mentioned this when he asked me to find a site for him. I did not understand her reasons, but one must respect anyone's feelings.

Henry Gross found some interesting information in different English pamphlets on water dowsing that he had read and put into practice. This evidently led him on to more experiments, with the result of great improvement and increased skills. Along this same line I have had occasion to receive amazing literature from England. They appear to have progressed far ahead of anyone else in the world. At present I find much of this progress to be way beyond my poor intellect, to fathom or understand, even though I am a true believer.

To get back to my own practical experiences,

I have gone from the forked branch to metal rods and the pendulum and, just recently, I have found, after many attempts and mistakes, that I can actually map dowse. My first try at this was when I was asked to go out to Mt. Gilead where a seven year old well had been turned down by the health department. The new owner needed a new site, so I asked the agent of the property for a plat or sketch (see map page 24) of the property indicating the boundary lines. He said he would leave one for me at his office the next morning. When I went to his office I met a friend who was associated with this agent and he said, "Dick, we were talking about your request for this plat and when it was explained you wished to dowse the map first before going out on the land, the first comment was, "Oh this is baloney!" I told my friend, "We shall see," and departed with the plat. That night I laid out the plat on a table and took my dowsing rod, a fork of young maple, and began slowly to traverse the boundary line of the seven acre tract. As the rod dipped at each place, I marked the spot with an X and upon completion I had five places marked. I then proceeded to connect the marks across the plat and found that they all went to one point on the south west corner of the property and then ran into the branch of the North Fork Creek, that ran into Goose Creek. I then checked the county soils book, which shows contour lines, streams and spring heads and lo and behold the courses I had marked on the plat corresponded exactly to the run of three streams, and where they met and ran as one was the identical place on the plat and soils book map. I was then able to ascertain the exact footage, using the scale of the plat, from the road frontage back into the property for each line of water crossing the tract. Having marked these distances on the plat, I was able, when I went onto the land, to pace off every one of the distances and then verify the exact spots with my dowsing rod. One place was about fifteen feet from the seven year old well that, had been turned down by the health department as being polluted and unfit for human consumption. The report was, it had a bad odor, a bad color and had a

22

high mineral content. I took my two angle rods and checked the polluted well. I asked if the underground vein of water in this well was good water, fit for human consumption. I got a "No" response. (A "Yes" answer to me is when the rods cross each other; with no movement for a "No" answer). I then asked the same question over the new site 15 feet away and got an immediate response. The rods crossed in a "Yes" answer. However, due to the close proximity of the polluted well, which had originally been good water seven years previously, we decided to discount this area. We established a site closer to the house, which indicated 11 gallons per minute at a depth of 150 feet. From now on I shall try to dowse on a plat, sketch or survey of the actual land before going onto the site. As this is my first attempt, I feel very excited about future events. I might add that it was the day before Christmas that I went to this property. The temperature was about 9 degrees and the wind chill factor, up on Mt. Gilead, was about 20 below zero. Although the owner, the agent and I moved about quickly,we were all very chilled. I got a severe cold in the head which turned into flu. It took six weeks for me to recover. However, all's well that ends well.

I have some very nice letters from people for whom I have helped to secure good water. One place in particular was a township, where there were three small sites at which to drill. Lucas Phillips asked me to go with him to see if I could help with the water shortage problem. We met the mayor and town engineer and I remember finding about 30 to 40 gallons per minute on two sites. But the third site was a gentle hill overlooking the surrounding township. It was used as the town's picnic area and there was a grove of large, old, original trees; oaks, maples and some big elms. I found a dome which was located in all directions from the hillock. Being some years ago I was not sure of depth or gallonage, but I knew there was a very strong flow. I heard later that they had drilled to 600 feet, gaining more water as they went down, and got 800 gallons per minute with no water problems since. Made me feel real good.

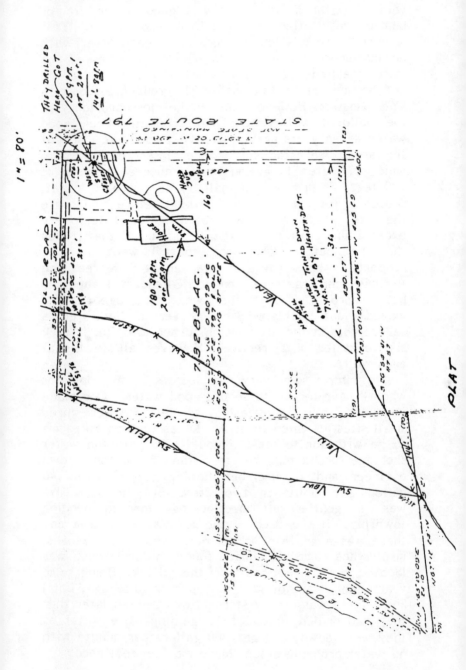

1" = 80'

PLAT

CHAPTER 3

EXPERIENCE IS THE BEST TEACHER

I acquired the book "Dowsing For Everyone" by Harvey Howells. It is excellent reading and I had a letter from Harvey later, remarking about my spelling of "cheque" which I used when I applied for his book. He said he had not seen that spelling in years. "Quite nostalgic", was his quote. He asked me what part of the Borders I call "home" and said he hailed from "dirty old Glasgow". It's probably as well he had only the word "cheque" to comment on, for if he read through any of my writings, he would, no doubt, find many more words of British spelling. I would recommend his book to everyone. It is very informative and to the point, in a simple manner that is appreciated and can be understood by a novice.

The pendulum has intrigued me but I still stay with the forked branch, though I believe the angle rods are now giving me more accurate readings in difficult areas. However I expect to be able to ask my forked branch more precise questions and get correct answers. Of course, as indicated, it is only with practice that assurance can be given. I must agree with all those before me when I am asked, "How does the dowsing rod work?" I say, "I don't know, but it does."

Possibly ten years ago Col. Heilman, an associate of mine, and I were out on a tract of land where a well site was required. After we had located a site, I said, "This vein runs on through the woods to the road, crosses the road to that house, and, I'll bet, their well is on the same vein". So we went over the road and a lady, whom Roland Heilman knew, was on the front lawn. He introduced me to her and I could see she was very pregnant. Roland asked her "when" and "did they want a boy or a girl?" The conversation finally got around to the pendulum and, as I had one in my pocket, I held if over her palm.

Soon it began to traverse back and forth in a straight line up and down her hand in line with her arm. I told her the baby would be a girl. Sure enough she had a lovely daughter. This has happened many times since for me and all of my predictions have been correct. When it is female over a female hand, the straight back and forth line is very true; but should the unborn be a male, there is the tendency for the pendulum to try to circle, but it is overcome by the adult female strength. If at this point the female hand is withdrawn and a male hand is put in it's place, the pendulum will only circle. If I hold the pendulum with my own right hand over my left palm, it will circle in a clockwise direction. If I change and hold the pendulum with my left hand over my right palm, it will go in a counter clockwise direction. As mentioned in Kenneth Roberts' book about Henry Gross, I'll bet, that if I could go into a barn where there were 100 cows bred in the fall to calve in the spring, I could be at least 90% correct as to what each one was carrying, a bull or heifer calf. My daughter and my wife both have felt the feeling of an electic shock or sharp prickling sensation when I tried the pendulum over their hands. Several other people have felt the same thing; some have said, "like pins and needles."

Harvey Howell's book makes a point regarding the angle rods and the location of north. I find this is no problem. No matter where I am, I can ask the rods to point to north, and as I circle around, the rods will cross evenly in the direction of north. I seem to be able to get more concrete answers from the rods than I do from the pendulum, though I still depend on, and always go back to, the forked branch, which, gradually is giving me more answers to my questions. I find that concentration, with no distraction, is essential along with the correct phrasing of the question.

There was one peculiar incident I recall with the dowsing rod. A lady was planning to build several houses in a small subdivision of 3 acre lots, septic systems and, of course, wells. So I was asked to find well sites for several of the initial lots. We met on

the land with her contractor, and also the well
driller, all of whom I knew. After the first sites were
located on each lot, the lady asked if she could try
her hand with the dowsing rod. After showing her the
usual way to hold the branch, I had her walk slowly
toward the last center I had marked. When she was
almost over the center, the rod went down and
continued on around, coming up between her arms
and she had to get her face out of the way quickly.
As it came up around, she could no longer hold the
ends as they finally slipped around in her hands.
Everyone was amazed, especially the lady, and she
has found several sites for others since that time. I
had that same thing happen once while I was dowsing
for a friend. We got 50 gallons of water per minute
at a depth of 50 feet and each time I went to the
center the rod would go down and then continue on
around and begin to come up toward my face. For
this I have no explanation.

The Leesburg Golf and Country Club has the
Tuscarora Creek running through the eighteen hole
course and in the central area there is a pond where
the creek flows in and out. Set up next to the pond
is a large pump, which operates the irrigation system
for the greens and fairways. Evidently the stream
and pond got so low on water that there was not
enough for the system. So they drilled close to the
pump to about 400 feet and got about 8 gallons per
minute. But they needed at least 40 gallons per
minute. One evening I got a phone call from the
owner, whom I knew, and he asked if I would go over
and try to select a good site for them. I asked who
told him to drill where he did. He said he just drilled
next to the pump thinking he would get enough.
Naturally I went to help and on scanning the area I
found I had to go further west away from the pump
and pond. As I got further away, with the well
drillers and owners watching me,the owner said, "We
don't want to get too far away from the pump as we
wish to use the same system." Well I said, "The water
is where the water is and not where your pump is".
So continuing west, I found that a considerable body
of water ran in a diagonal line across the golf course

in an opposite direction to Tuscarora Creek. Finally I decided on a spot about 100 yards from the pump and pond and, at a depth of 165 feet, at least 60 gallons of water per minute was located. I told them it would come to within 4 feet of ground level. The drillers gave me some peculiar looks and I felt the owners were very skeptical. But that night I noticed that the drill had been moved to the new location and a couple of days later it was gone from the area. I phoned the club and the owner's son spoke to me. I asked him what had taken place and he said, "Oh, Mr. Richards, it was great, we went down to 160 feet and got 65 gallons per minute and the water almost came up over the casing. It is now at 4 feet from ground level".

On the same property, I was asked to find a site for an emergency well at the Garden Apartments. On the 2 acre tract on the edge of the golf course, I picked up the same line of the diagonal flow found previously. It ran across the only piece of open ground of the 2 acres. At 225 feet, we got 125 gallons per minute. It was capped off and has not been used in 5 years.

Harry Lawson of Lucketts, near Leesburg, is a well driller of many years experience. He knows, from practice in this area, a great deal about the material through which he is drilling, rock, shale, sandstone, etc. and can tell by the chips and colors that come up, when and where he can expect to see water. Even though he has drilled many sites I have marked, he will not commit himself one way or the other regarding the dowsing rod. He admits he does get the feel of the rod but cannot explain it. I have known him to get his drilling rig into places one would have thought impossible. Some are dense wooded areas, with only the remote semblance of an age old logging trail, overgrown and hardly discernible. He cuts timber for a trail where he must, to get his big rig through. It is a big modern rig he operates, plus his big truck of drilling rods and spare parts and his water tank.

There are places that bear mentioning. One was north west of the town of Round Hill, at the end of a gravel road with a notice that read "END OF STATE MAINTENANCE". From that point, the narrow road climbed up into the Blue Ridge Mts. and about half a mile up this road was the property on which the well was needed. I had previously marked the site. I met "Buck" Lawson at the base of this climb. It was in February and we had just had a heavy snow storm. The main roads were plowed o.k., and the secondary county roads were passable, but at our meeting place the drifts were 4 feet deep and the narrow road up the mountain was full and drifted-in 3 feet deep. It was bitter cold. I said, "Buck, you will never get your rig up there. The lane is not much wider than your outfit". But in his quiet manner he said, "Aw I don't know, let's have a try and see". Well he plowed into the first drifts with his big rig in four wheel drive and, when he could no longer roll, he would back off and then forge into it again. So he continued up that climb with me following along behind on foot. It took about 1 1/2 hours to get to the property which was about 1/2 mile up. But he made it and, after I had shown him the spot, I was glad to leave. The well came in o.k. and everyone was happy.

The other occurance was here in Leesburg. Lucas Phillips (who is an attorney) had a client, an older lady, who had been told she must no longer drink chlorinated town water. She could cook with it, but must only drink pure water. She lived on one corner of a cross-street junction where there were all small lots with houses, etc, close together. I went to the property with Lucas and the only site I could find was on a 30 foot strip between the lady's house and the house next door. This location was slightly higher by about 2 feet than the neighbor's land. After marking the spot, I told Lucas there was about 30 plus gallons per minute at 100 feet depth. I said I could not see how a drilling rig could get to the spot due to sidewalk, shrubbery, trees and, especially the electric and telephone lines above. I had to leave town for several days and on my return, Lucas told me "Buck" Lawson succeeded alright, after some effort, and that the well came in at 40 gallons per minute and ran over into the garage of the house next door. I mention these two jobs to let the reader know, that generally these well drillers are pretty darn good fellows.

Over the past 12 months, well drillers have become busier than ever before and right now I believe there is a waiting period of about 4 to 6 weeks. Recently I heard on the news that, due to the general drought across the eastern states, where drilling companies usually have 10 to 15 calls a week, the number of calls has increased to 100 a week at times. I don't know how true it is, but I have heard that if the Hudson, Delaware and Potomac Rivers were bone dry, the cities of New York and Washington would have enough water in the reservoirs for only 48 hours. Makes one feel really dependent on nature and should give cause for serious thought. But knowing what I do about the general public, I don't suppose it will. It must be disasterville before they awaken. A fellow said to me the other day, "Hi Dick, how's it going?" I said, "Not too bad, but people are peculiar". He said, "I know what you mean, the more you deal with the public, the more you like your dog".

Last year I was able to acquire 3 different crude oil samples and I had always had an odd feeling about an area near here. It is a low lying tract of some 2,000 acres, with heavy clay subsoils, known locally as Black Jack area. Somehow, I have been drawn to this region and I went one day, on my own, along the roads through this location and did some quiet experiments. I could not get off the road and go onto the land as I did not have permission and did not wish to be caught trespassing and have to explain what I was doing. Therefore I did my dowsing at different spots along the roads.

30

DICK A. RICHARDS

CHAPTER 4

MORE THAN WATER

This period of dowsing for anything other than water was strange to me. But I did as I had read, and tipped the end of my young maple rod with a sample of the crude oil, which smelled strongly of tar or deisel oil. I kept coming back to one certain area, where a small stream ran under the road. From the northwest corner of the bridge over the stream, I had an insistant pull to the north and, after several times, I got the same answers. About 500 feet off the road in a pine-covered and scrub-covered area, the rod told me at 3,800 feet depth, there was a flow of 20 gallons per minute. This of course is 1,200 gallons per hour and 28,800 gallons per day. I don't know the gallonage of a barrel of oil, probably about 50 gallons. If so, I figured this would be 576 barrels per day. At $30.00 per barrel this would equal $17,180.00 per day. Of course, this is all incredible and I am only going on my feelings, possibly my imagination, but I had been strongly drawn to this section of the county for a long time. I don't know why, but I had to go and see. The above results are what the rod gave me. I have not talked to anyone about this, as I am not sure. I don't know the slightest thing about areas that would show an indication of oil and what oil people look for or how much volume is required to make drilling worthwhile. I believe I will try to get another opinion and go over again what I have done.

From my home in the evening, I have tried some long distance dowsing and in one particular instance, I tried to prove to myself it's accuracy. About two weeks ago, I went to a crushed stone company to find a well site for them, and as you can imagine, a quarry area is generally solid rock base. However I found a vein that ran right under one of their newer buildings, which, at 270 feet, showed a flow of 11 gallons per minute. About a mile away, on another tract, where they were going to build a couple of houses, I marked another site for them, 150 feet deep and 6 gallons per minute. I know they are drilling but I have not heard from them as yet. So from inside my house, I have held my rod and, after explaining the exact location, I ask if water was found at 270 feet. I got a "Yes" answer. Then I asked if the well was more than 270 feet deep, again "Yes". Finally at 380 feet down I got a flow of 22 gallons per minute. So I am waiting to see what they actually did.

At the same time, in my home, I held up my rod and, pointing in the general direction of the area where I checked for oil, I gave the approximate distance and location and asked, "Is there oil underground in this area at 4,000 feet below the surface?" The rod indicated "Yes." Would the flow, when tapped, be 20 gallons per minute?" The answer was "Yes." Please don't ask me how, why, when, if or what. I don't know. Concerning water,I am sure when the rod says it is so, it has been proven in practice and results. But oil dowsing is something different and, in fact, coupled with distance, it becomes somewhat scary. Another thing I notice, I feel much more tense and nervous when asking questions regarding oil. I don't mean excited. I mean physically tense. This is all very peculiar and mystifying. I have come to the conclusion that one needs proof. So I shall ask my friend, Lucas Phillips, to be with me and maybe we can devise a plan that will prove my actions and the actions of the rod. I will at least have witness to what occurs.

One is led deeper into dowsing. Henry Gross would have his rod tell him how many people were in a certain house hundreds of miles away. He could tell how many people were in the house, how many were males and how many were females. I believe, in the book "Dowsing for Everyone", by Harvey Howells, the dowsing rod tracked correctly, a young man's journey across half of the United States. I am now trying this experiment with a trip being made by my daughter and son-in-law who live in Maryland about 50 miles from us. Without them knowing, I am practicing asking my rod, if they are home together, if only one of them is home and, if so, which one. I am also checking times etc. Later, when my wife talks to our daughter by phone, I will have her quiz our daughter as to where they were and at what times etc. Then I can go from that, if correct, to more detailed and proven experiments.

I have gone outside our house, knowing that my wife, Barbara, was indoors, and asked my rod if she was on the ground floor or the second floor. Once I had a "No" for the ground floor and a "Yes" for the second floor. But at that moment another light came on upstairs. All of this needs more proof positive. I am not about to ask scientists their opinions. They would probably ridicule the whole thing, and after seeing my typing or reading my initial writings, they would probably say, "How can one expect to even consider an opinion of a man who can't even spell".

I have several letters, from happy clients, which I will attach to this writing. I shall ask all of those for whom I find water in the future, to write me their feelings and I will keep a file on their comments.

I believe that as there are great bodies of oil, gas, liquid chemicals and subteranian movements within the earth, so there could be vast bodies of water also. The domes of water that rise in the hills are independent bodies that do not depend on rain fall or the outer atmosphere for their quanity or flow. I think the outer surface of our earth does depend naturally on rainfall, but it has been written that a large underground river flows beneath the Sahara Desert and I have known of very severe droughts in the lower valleys, when nearby mountain springs and wells flow at their usual rate.

I had one instance as manager of a farm in New Jersey, when we had about 200 acres which we irrigated for brome and alfalfa crops only. We had two one-acre spring-fed ponds, where we had a 1200 gallon per minute pump. One particular year, 1956 or 1957, there was a very bad drought. Surrounding farms of market garden produce and grains, that depended on rainfall only, were burned out. People came to see our 3rd and 4th crops of heavy legume which were 3 feet high. We had the only green patch in the district. The water level of the ponds did drop a little, but evidently the source of the springs from underground did not show any effect of the drought. Perhaps my idea is questionable, but the rivers do receive their supply, originally, from the mountains. The mountain springs, domes and streams do not receive their supply from the rivers in the lowlands. Surely then, this mountain water must come from existing sources within the earth.

In dowsing the domes of water in Bermuda, Henry Gross found that one dome rose to within 30 feet of ground level and produced 80 gallons per minute. Also that this source came from a depth of 3,500 feet, which was far below sea level. I question the fact that this source of water is supplied by rain.

At another point in Bermuda, Henry Gross marked a site 59 feet above sea level. When the drill reached the 77 foot mark, 18 feet below sea level, there was 3 feet of water in the hole. At 80 feet, there was 7 1/2 feet of water and no trace of salt, just good clean drinkable water.

Is it possible during a drought period, when the whole surface of the earth is in need of water, that a heavy rain can replenish the ground surface, raise pond and stream level, freshen crops and vegetation and also soak down 300 to 400 feet to replenish deep underground sources? Or would even the heaviest rain be used up and gone before it could reach 200 feet deep into the parched soil? On January 26, 1981, Gordon Barnes, TV weather forecaster, related the seriousness of the drought which is taking place in our entire eastern states area. No doubt 2 or 3 inches of steady rain would eleviate this situation and the reservoir would fill up again. But if we were to go, immediately into another dry spell, in two months the situation could be worse than before.

I spoke or wrote previously of the increase in our country's population over the next ten years being double that of the previous ten years. Such increases are occurring all over the country, not just in one county. Therefore, unless there is a drastic reduction in the use of water (or the waste of it) or that considerable measures are taken to acquire and reserve more quantities of clean water, very critical situations will arise. In the future even minor droughts might cause the authorities' present requests for no car washing, no lawn sprinkling, less toilet flushing, shorter showers, and water served in restaurants only by request, to seem very minor in comparison. I would even go as far as to say I believe the day is not far away when water will be much more important than oil. It always has been, although the fact has not been recognized in the initial scheme of life.

Our industrial, scientific complex of modern life styles demand that we have abundant oil, gas, electricity, coal, power and enormous energy. Yet in times past, the only basic need for all other living things, both animal and vegetable, was WATER. It also applies that, in our production of all the great energy we need, we use water to wash, clean, propel and produce, by the trillions of gallons daily, which when used and polluted by chemicals etc. is washed away into the rivers and then to the sea.

Through all of this, Joe Blunt's well, on his 50 acre farm, still produces it's original 10 gallons per minute, of good clean water for his family and livestock. Edgar Cayce wrote, "The man on the side of the mountain with good green grass and a clean spring of water will be the millionaire of the future".

CHAPTER 5

LETTERS, I GET LETTERS....

In this chapter are over a dozen letters from clients whom I have been able to help. It makes me feel good to receive these appreciations, knowing that one is able to help one's fellow man, with great enjoyment, dignity and thankfulness for having been granted the ability through nature, to use the dowsing rod and find sources of water.

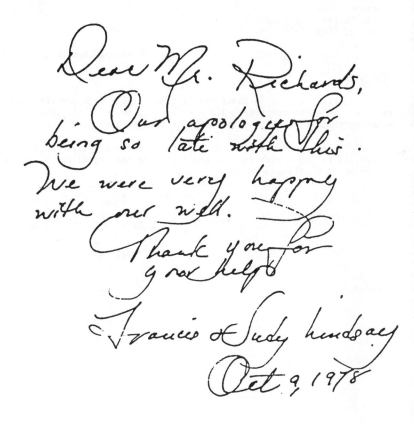

the magna group inc.

September 18, 1978

Mr. Dick Richards
Myers-Building
184 E. Market Street
Leesburg, Virginia 22075

Re: Leesburg Country Club Sect. IV

Dear Dick:

First I want to thank you for taking your time and skill locating water on the above property. Since that time, the town has taken off the water mortorium; and we decided to go to public water.

I am enclosing a check for $200.00 for our appreciation. I will be getting in touch with you as soon as I know the septic field status on the property I told you about.

Sincerely,

Robert O. Lehmann/cab
Vice President

ROL/cab
Enclosure.

I. L. HOYLE, JR.

ROUND HILL, VIRGINIA 22141
December 15, 1978

Mr. Dick A. Richards
Box 367
Leesburg, Va. 22075

Dear Mr. Richards

Thank you for your water divining service on my lots
in Round Hill, Virginia.

In reviewing the well sites the following table best
describes the results.

SITE NO.	DICK RICHARDS FORCAST	ACTUAL RESULTS
#1	85 ft. to 100 ft. 8 to 10 GPM 12 ft. from ground	93 ft. 19-20 GPM 12 ft. 3 inches
#2	100 ft. to 110 ft. 10-12 GPM 9 ft. from gound	107 ft. 13 GPM 10 ft. 3 inches
#3	125 ft. to 130 ft. 12-14 GPM 15 ft from ground	67 ft. 4.5 GPM 9 ft. 9 inches

Enclosed is my check per our agreement and again I would
like to thank you.

Very truly yours

I. L. HOYLE, JR.

39

Nick Greer
Antique Restoration

ANTIQUES
FINE FINISHES
CUSTOM FURNITURE
WOODCARVING
MINIATURE FURNITURE

ROUTE 2. BOX 208M
PURCELLVILLE. VA 22132
703/338-6607

Dear Mr. Richards

Thank you for your help. We
are enjoying our water out of our
artesian well —

Sincerely
Nick Greer

4-6-79

Dear Dick,

We got 100 gal to the minute
at 200 ft. at the old farmhouse
site you staked for us. Buck Lawson
drilled the well for us.

Many Thanks
Ed Cross
Tri-County Coast, Inc.

5/23/79

Dick:

160 feet, 12 gallon
per minute –

Thanks –

Bud Droege
tel. 301/453-1683

(P.S. – I lost your card –
if this check is made
out incorrectly to the
extent you can't cash
it, let me know & I'll
correct it.

(In case you don't recall –
you estimated 150 feet
and 9-10 GPM)

Brookfield Farm
June 21, 1979

Forecast : 1 65-180' - 8-10 gal

Results : 12 to 15 gal. per minute
at 110 ft. drilled.

Amount of Storage : (1½ gal. per ft in casing)

Dick:

Really appreciate your coming
out to the farm to help locate
the well. Your forecast was
right on the money; only we didn't
have to drill as deep as you thought.

Thanks again

Bill Harrison

Route 2, Box 170-B
Leesburg, Virginia   22075

Dick A. Richards
Leesburg, Virginia   22075
July 1, 1979

Dear Mr. Richards,

I must say I had my doubts when you came to locate the
site for our well. You predicted that at 60 ft. we would be
getting one to two gallons per minute, and at 120-140 ft. we
would be getting 10 to 12 gallons per minute.

The finished well produced 25 gallons per minute at 165 ft.
The water level is 16 ft. from the ground, and you predicted 20 ft.
from ground level.

We are well pleased and appreciate you help in locating
water.

        Respectfully yours,

        Robert Maxwell

2-3-81

Tommy W. Owen
Rt. 1 Box 128 A
Chantilly, Va. 22021

Dear Mr. Richards,

Since our meeting in July, I
had a well drilled at the spot you
picked out for me just below the
garage. You predicted I would get
4-5 gal. per minute at 165 ft and
that the water would come to within
14-15 ft. of the top. I actually got
about 1 pint per minute at 165 ft. and
the water came to within 11ft. of the
top.

An interesting change took place
though. Within three weeks time the
water evidently started breaking-in as
we were no longer draining the well.
In fact, since September we have not been
able to drain off the water despite a
prolonged drought period and our own
heavy usage.

Therefore we are sending a check for your
fee and our thanks for making our house our home.
Sincerely, Tommy W. Owen

44

9-4-81

Nick -

Sorry for the delay and the fact I can only send $25.00 now. Believe me I will send $50.00 more as soon as I can!

You said we would hit water in the area you selected at 110 feet and the flow would be 10 to 12 gpm and the water would rise to 18' from ground level. I must admit, at the time, I had no confidence in your method, but since I figured you knew more than I, we drilled exactly where you told us to.

Fortunately for my nerves, Randy had Mr. Hanson drill when I was not there. He went down to 180 feet and still no water, at 190 feet he hit 2 gpm, at 240 feet he hit FIFTY gpm and he stopped at 250 feet where he "estimated" 60 yes SIXTY gpm. He (Mr. Hanson) said it was probably more, but his hose filled a 5 gal. bucket before he could count more than to 2 or 3!

Now I am so happy to have that kind of flow

rate, that I couldn't believe it was a "chance" occurrance. I am now a believer in you and your method and you can show this letter to anyone, however, a sceptic may think you dreamed it up. By-the-way the water has since risen to 28 feet from ~~ground level!~~

We have a tremendous reservoir! - approx 350 gallons. This is truly a great well, especially since we have a 1/4 acre garden and plan to build a swimming pool. The Town of Round Hill would love to have my well!

Another interesting thing is that I accurately measured the well myself. I measured to 275' and still did not hit bottom. Since the well was only drilled 250' I speculate we are in a large river or lake. You won't remember, but you showed us at the time you were there where a "vein of water" ran and what direction it flowed.

Do you have any explanation for the fact that the water was actually 80 feet or so deeper than you thought?? However, the flow far exceeded your predictions. I have been told we actually have enough water for a small community!

Thanks again & happy "hunting." When my Mom & Dad build their house, hopefully next year, I will give you a call.

I hope this will provide some info for your book. I still wonder if the dead mouse you found had anything to do with this??!!

PETER RANDOLPH HOLDEN
33 ROCK SPRING DRIVE
LEESBURG, VIRGINIA 22075

May 1, 1981

Dear Dick,

Thank you again for your help in locating water on my lot. Please excuse my procrastination in sending this letter — the time has just flown by since I began this endeavor.

As I mentioned earlier Singhas hit water at 175 feet at the rate of 4 gallons / minute. The final depth of the hole is 265 feet which gives me plenty of reservoir. Your estimate was 6-8 gal./min. at 150 ft. with a possible 10-12 gal/min at 250+ ft.

I am pleased with the results and I have enclosed my payment to you. At this point in time I am planning on keeping my townhouse as an investment. If I change plans I will contact you.

Thank you again,
Peter

48

5/10/81

Dick

Drilling 300' and not finding the water you expect is a traumatic experience. Therefore, I very much appreciate your prompt trip out when I called you to select a new drilling site.

Thanks for the dowsing instructions you gave me and letting me work with you to find a new drilling site. It is an experience I will never forget.

I would love to read your manuscript.

Andy Pitas

49

CHAPTER 6

HOW TO BEGIN

I wonder if I can explain to the would be dowser, in simple terms, how to be begin?

#1 Be serious about what you are attempting and concentrate on the imaginary picture you have in your mind of an underground stream or vein of water; think of clear crystal water.

#2 Select a forked branch of young wood, that is as follows:

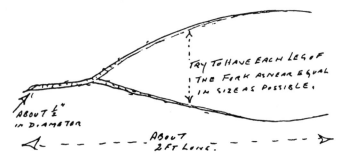

TRY TO HAVE EACH LEG OF THE FORK AS NEAR EQUAL IN SIZE AS POSSIBLE.

ABOUT ½" IN DIAMETER

ABOUT 2 FT LONG.

Holding your hands palms up, place each leg of the fork across each palm and under the thumbs. Grip with each hand, holding the point of the fork upward at about 45 degrees. Keep your elbows at about waist height, slightly away from your body. Relax your body and concentrate on water running below ground.

#3 You are outside on an open tract of land. Regardless of where you are standing, begin to circle, very slowly to your right. Try to feel any movement the forked branch makes. If you feel any slight downward pull, stop. Then reverse your direction, going back in a circle to your left, slowly. Feel again and if you find another pull to your left, stop and consider your situation. Did the pulls to right and left go far enough each way as

to feel that the strength of pull was more
to the rear, or was it more to the
front. This should give you a sense of the
location and the direction. When you think
you know, mark the line on the ground
with a couple of stones or sticks. So far,
you have used 180 degrees or one half of
a 360 degree circle. Now begin at the
center, turn your back on that half you
already scanned and do the same procedure on the other 180 degrees. Again
mark the line. You may have used two
lines marked, as follows:

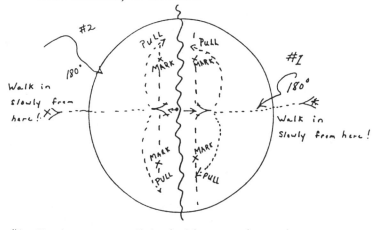

#4 Having accomplished this, stand at what
you consider to be the center of your imaginary circle. Then pace away at right
angles to the lines you marked, to the
outer edge of your circle. Go about 20
paces, turn around and face the center
again. Hold up your forked branch in the
correct position and slowly retrace your
steps toward the center. At the first
indication of any downward pull, stop.
Mark that spot on the ground then hold
your fork in position again. You will find
it will not move. However as you begin
again to move forward to the center it
will show movement and will go down
completely over the center. Do this same

51

thing again from the opposite outer edge of the circle. Again mark the first movement down and then center. You will find that the distance, from the center to the first marker, is exactly the same on each side and you have found "center".

#5 If, at first, you get no response, do not be disappointed, but continue to try in other areas. Keep your mind open and generally it is better to be on your own in the beginning. Later when you have felt the power of the dowsing rod, it might be good to have a friend with you to witness and verify your findings.

Some time ago, Tom Hatcher called me and said they had trouble at Oatlands Plantation, just south of town. It appeared that at one of the residences, a leaking fuel-oil tank had polluted their well. They had decided to drill at a lower spot below the house, just across the main driveway, which they did, I was told, on the advise of a geologist who said there was abundant water at 50 feet in that particular area. But they were down about 250 feet and had found no water. So I went with Tom to check with the drillers. They were at 265 feet and dry, so I began to scan the area and found, according to my rod that there was 16 gallons per minute, at the spot they were drilling, at a depth of 270 feet. They were about to give up and move to another site, but I told Tom and the driller that they were about to hit water. I could see the driller did not believe me, but Tom told them to continue a few more feet. We waited and watched and after about 20 minutes or so, the driller called us over and said, "We have hit water and the flow is getting stronger." I believe they went on down to about 280 feet and got 27 gallons per minute.

There was one experience which I cannot understand. I was called to a farm near Hagerstown, Maryland, where over a period of years, nine wells had been drilled. One or two were giving enough water for the house and buildings, but enough was needed for a considerable number of wintered livestock. I did not know the history of the place before I got there and, at that time, I was not knowledgable enough to do map dowsing. However, of two sites I located neither were successful and they eventually drilled in a low area near a dried out stream bed and found about 20 gallons per minute. I feel I was distracted that day, as four or five people were around me all the time and there were some pretty flippant remarks and jokes flying around. This is really no excuse and it is my intention to get a plat of this property and see if I can find, through map dowsing, a good source of water for them. I would like to do this and refute the smart alec remarks that have since been made, but one can always expect ridicule from some people. Those same people are silent about many previous successes, even though they participated in the benefits. I agree that a good dowser must be correct all the time, but I believe there are certain circumstances which, if rechecked, would prove the reversal of some initial apparent failures. I have found out since that one of the two sites I marked, now has water and the other was not used because the health department would not approve the location.

Once I had a call from a company in Washington, that had acquired a fifty acre tract of land which they intended to develop and they needed to locate sites for 140 wells. On the telephone, I asked, "What are the sizes of the lots?" I was told they were 1/4 acre each. I answered, "You better forget your project right now. You must understand you do not have a lake under your fifty acres, where you can just drill down and hit water at any spot. There are veins and streams of water running underground and they take the point of least resistance in their travels. So on a tract of fifty acres, there may be one, two or more veins crossing the tract and, where they run, wells can be drilled. But of the fifty acres, it is possible that only twenty acres may have underground water, which, in turn, might only supply 4 or 5 wells." After further conversation I suggested, that when they were in the area, they should stop in and see me and we could discuss their situation in more detail. This they did within a few days. It appeared that in order for them to begin construction, they must guarantee that they could supply water. The guarantee was necessary before the loan or banking companies would consider construction loans. At that particular time, there was a moratorium, by the town, concerning the supply of town water. This was due to dry weather and a short water supply and, even though the developers had planned to put in a complete system of pipe lines as required by the town, with all the necessary meters etc., they still had to show a sufficient water supply. After hearing their predicament, I advised them, since their land ran to the foothills and partially up into a section of the Catoctin Mountain Range, to find two or three sites at the highest points that could supply about 30 to 40 gallons per minute or a possible total of 4,800 gallons per hour, 115,200 gallons per day. That should be enough for the daily requirement of 1,000 people, at 100 gallons per person. They could, by using a couple of pumps, run it through their planned town pipe system until town water was available Then they would have an excellent reserve system, or additional system, if needed at any time. I had the impression that they comprehended and they agreed with no hesitation.

One of the partners and I met on the land and in scanning the higher ground along the fifty acres, among the brush and undergrowth, I found three sites. One was at each end and one about the center, along the high boundary line. Both of the end sites would produce about 40 gallons per minute, at a depth of about 200 plus feet. The center site was only about 12 gallons per minute. The young engineer partner who accompanied me was delighted and we marked the site with stakes and sprayed red paint over six inches of the stake tops.

Naturally I was delighted to be able to help them and, also, that they had taken my advise. It was simple advise that had gotten them what they required and after we had gone over possible costs and time saved, it had saved them about $500,000.00. They did not drill either well, as soon afterwards, the town removed the moratorium and supplied their water needs. So there are two good sites still there to be used when they are needed.

I received a very nice letter from these young fellows and they said it had been a pleasant experience and expressed their sincere appreciation. I always walk around feeling a little taller, with a nice feeling inside, after such events and it helps me to sleep at night.

A few weeks ago I had occasion to visit a quarry and crushed stone establishment. I was asked by the owner to select a well site for them. They had a well which produced about 2 or 3 gallons per minute and near it there was a water tower with a tank above, from which gravity fed the water to the different offices and buildings. They now needed a greater supply, as they were expanding. In particular they wanted a supply closer to a new building, where they had plans for additional constuction and roadway. I guessed the building to be about 100' x 200'. As usual I scanned the area and, as I did so, I could see, all around me, the grey, rocky, stone surface of the land. There was dusty powder from the stone everywhere, as one would expect in a quarry and crushed stone operation. It was a barren-looking location with big trucks moving in and out; a busy place. I thought there wouldn't be many, if any, veins running through that rock. However after a short time, I changed my opinion. A vein ran from the front of the building, diagonally across one end, out a rear corner, across the road and on past a storage area for large metal oil and chemical drums. The owner, a young foreman and several other men had arrived, very curious to see the water dowser. Several remarks were made, such as, "My grandfather used to be able to find water with a peach branch" and, "What type stick do you use?" etc. I showed some of them how to hold the rod and it worked for one of them, much to the delight of his friends. The owner, on whose farm I had located a well some years before, said, "Of course it works; it works for me. I tried it years ago with Mr. Richards." Anyway, the place I marked was across the road, close to the drum storage area, but they decided, among them, that later they would want to utilize this section for an additional road and parking space. So they asked me if I could locate a spot closer to the building, and after checking it out I said, "Yes" and that at 270 feet there was water and it would produce 11 gallons per minute. The following sketch shows where the vein ran.

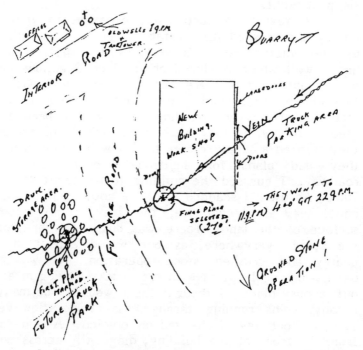

I finally left the quarry and, later, I heard they had begun to drill and had gone down about 40 feet and would continue to drill.

I heard no more from them for a while and one night I became curious to know what was happening. I took my rod, in my living room here in my house, and holding it up, and after giving the location and name of the place, I asked, "At the well site at the corner of the new building, is the underground vein of water good pure water, fit for human consumption?" The rod indicated "Yes." I then asked, "Is there water 270 feet deep?" The answer was "No." Then I asked, "Is there water at 300 feet?"

CHANTILLY CRUSHED STONE,
DIVISION OF PERCONTEE, INC.

Box 112, Chantilly, Virginia 22021 • Quarry Location 4 miles west of Chantilly on U.S. Route 50

CRUSHED STONE FOR ALL PAVING & CONSTRUCTION   telephone 471-4461 • 703 FAirview 7-6333

February 9, 1981

Mr. Dick A. Richards
Box 367
Leesburg, Va. 22075

Dear Mr. Richards:

I am writing to you in connection with the Services you rendered
to us in connection with determining the Best possible location for
drilling a new Well here at our plant.

I well remembered the Success I had as a result of your Services
in locating a well at my residence up on Mt. Gilead. This time I
felt that you would really be challenged in helping us determine
where to drill, because of the fact we are in a Stone Quarry and all
of our land is underlain with solid rock. At the time that I called
you, we already had two existing wells outside of our office, both of
which had been drilled without the benefit of your services; and,
both of which after many hundreds of feet in depth only produced
1 gallon per minute. The location that you chose for our new well at
the shop building brought in a well with 20 gallons per minute, which
was very, very pleasing to us.

I am not very Knowledgeable regarding the 'Dowsing" techniques,
however, with your instructions both my employees and myself were able
to unquestionably experience the "down-turning" of the forked branch
that was held in our hands when we approached the location that you had
chosen as being the spot for us to drill our well. With the success that
we had, we find no question marks or doubts left to our thinking.

Thanking you for your services, please find enclosed our check in
payment as per agreement. Thank you.

Very truly yours,

ARNOLD BORTMAN

AB/pmd
Encl.

NORTHERN VIRGINIA'S LARGEST PRODUCER OF CRUSHED STONE

57

The answer was "Yes." Then, "Will this vein of good water flow at 11 gallons per minute at a 300 foot depth?" The answer was "No." "Will it flow at 5 gallons per minute?" The answer, "Yes." "At 6 gallons per minute?" The answer, "Yes." "At 8 gallons per minute?" The answer "No." So I was satisfied with 6 to 7 gallons per minute. Then after questioning the rod I found that at a depth of 380 feet it flowed at 20 gallons per minute.

After some time had passed and I had not heard what had happened at the site, I phoned and spoke with the owner. He said, "Oh Mr. Richards at 270 feet the driller said there was very little water, so we drilled deeper and at about 300 feet we had water. We continued and got more and at 400 feet we got 20 gallons per minute. We are very happy." I told him I was very glad for him, and pointed out that this was 1200 gallons per hour and 28,000 gallons per day. He laughed and said, "We've never had so much water and we shall try to live with it." He is sending me a letter which I will enter into this writing.

I have attempted my first real long range dowsing and I feel somewhat awed by the results. I have been able to go onto a tract of land and tell the direction and whereabouts of water up to a couple of hundred yards. But this event has me nervously excited and I have tried this on other sites I have located and have gotten answers, but have not proven them, as yet. However I am becoming addicted and will continue to experiment.

I am about to try out the rod on humans and hope I can verify the number of people that may be within a certain building, or home, at a given time and, if this can be proven, as Henry Gross proved it, it will be an astonishing feat. I wonder sometimes if I should be satisfied finding well sites and water, because this can become not necessarily scary, but rather strange, to the point whereby a dignified, respectful and even reverant attitude must be applied. It is certainly not to be considered a plaything and, I feel, must never be taken advantage of.

CHAPTER 7

MR. RICHARDS! HELP!

It is not my intention in these writings, to say what should or should not be, or to give the impression that I am of such great learning that my knowledge and source of information, is impeccable and therefore fact. Rather I am relating experiences and at the same time asking questions which I feel are from the standpoint of common sense, that in turn may have the tendency to make others, who are interested in dowsing, ask similar questions, thereby acquiring answers and more knowledge.

It seems to me that the extent to which the power that controls the dowsing rod can go, is limitless. I don't know what this power is, but as it is so powerful a part of nature and over many, many years a proven fact, which appears to lead to greater discoveries by some very eminent people, scholars, scientists and doctors alike, that in a more quiet and perhaps much more beneficial way, it could very well outclass the atomic energy period in which we now live. Anyway mankind is racing ahead, with unbelievable new discoveries being brought to light daily and what was considered to be entirely impossible 25 years ago, has come about and even surpassed the initial belief. We may live to see the awesome powers of nature, as yet having only the surface scratched, being more easily understood and used in a simple manner, for the world and humanity. Man has not yet been able to equal the destructive power of lightning, earthquakes, floods, fire, tornados, hurricanes and typhoons. Nor has he been able to manufacture such events as the birth of a rosebud and it's blooming, the eternal growth of grass underfoot, the growth in the womb of human or animal and the procedure of birth. We take these quiet natural things for granted. As I related in the beginning of these writings, among all of the above we see the interwoven pattern of water commonplace, natural, taken for granted and yet it's whereabouts, course, quantity etc. can be ascertained by the forked branch from a tree in the hands of a human. Water is one of the great powerful forces in nature.

Is it possible that the other great powers of nature are really very simple to diagnose and perhaps utilize? If this is the case, we would not need inventors or scientific mechanical wonders. We would be on a balance with nature. Well, it may come to pass. Stranger things have already happened.

I have noted several times, incidences where the original prediction was, for example, 8 gallons per minute at a well site. After the well was drilled the actual gallons per minute were 6 gallons. Then within 48 hours the missing 2 gallons came through and the total 8 gallons per minute flowed. This situation seems to depend on the type of material the drill bit is cutting into, if it is shale or gravel. The full amount of water is there when the drilling is completed, but if the bit is cutting through rock or fragmented rock, there is the tendency for the vein or veins to be sealed off, as the drill bit makes a cement-like mixture, which forms a seal. But after 48 to 76 hours, the vein forces it's way around and then through the sealed off areas and washes itself free, to run again on it's original course. As Henry Gross said, "A twenty ton bulldozer will crush the outlet of a spring or vein, so that it will turn, find another course and take the path of least resistance." That is why, years ago, when a vein was found close to the surface and a well shaft was hand dug, and once the main flow was established, the walls of the shaft were lined with stone, laid so that water could flow through the openings between the stones, like a stone wall fence row. There are not many areas here that I know of, where a well can be hand dug. Anyway, nowadays young men won't or don't know how. Forty to fifty feet is the minimum depth and the average is about 175 feet. Many must go to 300 or 400 feet, so it is much easier to use a mechanical drill, with the upper 50 feet having a 6" or 8" steel pipe casing, grouted in with concrete, in some instances. The authorities require a 100 foot casing.

Last night, I had a telephone call from a

young man for whom I found a well site about a year ago. The results were to be 160 feet deep, 6 gallons per minute and the water should rise to within 12 feet of ground level. After drilling to 200 feet, they had only 1 gallon per minute and, at that time, I told him the water was there and it would come in after the veins had cleared themselves. Anyway I heard nothing from him all last year, until last night. He said, "Mr. Richards I am very sorry to call you so late. I wanted to write to you but I lost your address. Several days after we drilled the well, I went and checked, and in taking the cap off the casing, I could see the water. With a string and a weight I measured the distance and it was 15 feet from the top of the casing, which was 2 1/2 to 3 feet above ground; so your figure of 12 feet from ground level was correct. We decided the full flow must have come in, so we had a pump fitted and we know we are getting more than 6 gallons per minute. We have had no shortage of water all summer and fall. During the drought, over the last six months, people around us have had to be careful with their use of water, while we have used all we need, inside and outside too." He apologized again for the long delay and said he would write me a letter to confirm his appreciation for the help I had given them. I explained to him that this type of situation often happens and, given time and patience, the veins clear the restrictions and come back. He told me he would recommend me to any of his friends and I said if I could help him in the future to let me know.

My wife said what a difference there is in people; that young man is appreciative and evidently has character and principal. Naturally I had to agree with her. I had forgotten about him and it was nice to hear from him. The opposite of the above personage was the chap who was about to build a $150,000.00 home on ten acres he had just acquired. I went to his tract of land with him and he showed me where he intended to lay out his house site and also the septic field. After scanning the site, I found a spot which was very suitable for him in all respects and it was, I recall, at 170 feet depth and 7 gallons per minute. Having marked the site for him, I left and over the next few months, whenever I drove by the area, I saw that his house was under construction and progressing rapidly. But I noticed no well had been drilled. One day I drove onto the property and over the spot I had marked was a big pile of lumber and materials. A couple of men were there, working on the plumbing and electrical fittings in the basement. During a chat with them I found that the house would soon be finished, but the well had not been drilled. Some time later the owner came to see me and told me they had drilled but they had to go to 200 feet and only got 4 to 5 gallons per minute. So as my predictions were wrong, he felt he owed me nothing. I told him I was glad he had finally drilled and that he had 240 gallons per hour, which would be more than he would ever need and wished him, "Good luck." Being very excited about his new home, he went on to say, "I want you to come and see my home, Mr. Richards, it's a wonderful floor plan. You know I spent $500.00 on the colored glass in the front door alone". At this point I felt like telling him, "There is the door, get out". Of course I did not and I did not go to see this wonderful expensive home either.

While dowsing and traveling around our county in my spare time, I have found indications, in several areas, of large quantities of water underground. Of course until they are needed, they will remain underground and it is not possible to convey these locations to anyone. Unless people are in dire need, they do not believe.

The members of a Virginia township asked me to check out a certain area for them some years ago. They had already drilled several wells at considerable cost. After spending a couple of days in the particular area, I told those in charge that the best they could expect was an average of about 80 gallons of water per minute, at about the 400 foot depth, anywhere on that tract. But there was 300 to 400 gallons per minute at that same depth in certain areas around the town and if they would get permission to go onto the land, I would be happy to help. But I had no response from them. Sometime later I heard that, again, those in charge, had been asked by an official of the town, "Why didn't you get Mr. Richards to continue to help?". The answer was, "We felt it was not scientific." Some time later they did drill in an area I had indicated and hit two lovely supplies, one at 500 gallons per minute and one about 400 gallons per minute. They did eleviate their water problem and, of course, they were all smiles. The person who has a houseful of week-end guests and calls and says, "Can you help us immediately? Please, our spring has gone dry, we can't wash, bathe, or even wash-up the dishes. Could you come now?" A site is found, the drill is on the way, a tank of water is supplied to tide them over, the well comes in with plenty of good, cold water. Every one is happy and much more understanding than the skeptical, closed mind that must have scientific facts.

CHAPTER 8

WATER, THANK GOD!

The value of water or any other commodity, is not, and has never been, appreciated and will not be until it is nonexistant. As stated previously, water throughout the ages is priority number one.

I have never been in a desert, but I have a very vivid imagination of what it must be like, to be lost in such terrain, with no water. I know what a severe drought can do to crops and livestock. I have had that experience first hand. Everyone has seen in pictures or TV, the plight of many African tribes on the move, in search of grazing for their livestock and water for their families. The horrible circumstances in such situations cannot be understood unless actually experienced or seen. I have often wondered why it is not possible to have well drilling rigs working in such areas, so that a line or chain of wells could be drilled along a route. We have run railway lines across continents and over and under mountain ranges. Surely at stops, villages or camps along an often traveled route, well sites could be found and drilled. I know that multitudes of people would kneel and say, "WATER---THANK GOD."

Miss Penrose who was mentioned in Kenneth Robert's book on Henry Gross, must have been a very remarkable lady. I would imagine her exploits, particurarly in Africa, were miraculous. She must have brought great comfort to thousands, by her wonderful dowsing abilities. Also such a lady must have enjoyed great comfort upon seeing the faces of those for whom she found water.

When you can take a drink of water leisurely whenever you need it and the water is always there, it becomes meaningless. No thought is given to the possibility of it not being there and each of us can drink in peace with no concern. But when hundreds or thousands of humans are without water and all thirsty at the same time and many even dying of thirst, they become a mob of wild, crazed things all needing desperately to drink at once, even to the point of killing each other to get water. I experienced this once with 170 head of Hereford cattle, which were in comfortable winter quarters, with electrically operated water tanks in each building. Any one of the cattle could drink as they wished, which they did, so that never was there more than one or two drinking at the same time. As the water was drunk and the levels dropped, the ball cocks opened and water flowed in. There were no problems and every animal was satisfied.

Suddenly one night in February 1957, near Moorerstown, New Jersey, we had a very heavy fall of snow. It was of the large flake, wet variety, which came very quickly and in heavy volume all night. Tree limbs, telephone and electrical lines were torn down with the weight of the snow and, all around the district, transformers on large electrical poles would short out with big blue flashes. A widespread area was without electricity and repair crews came from other states to help get things back to normal. It was several days before power was completely supplied, and during that period, we had to haul water in mobile tanks, 50 gallon drums on wagons and tractors, for the 170 head of cattle. It was a day and night operation and it seemed almost impossible to satisfy their thirst. The bawling of those animals could be heard for miles and they would climb over each other to get to the water each time we came with another load. We managed to keep going and finally the power came back on, but I never want to see a similar situation again. I can readily imagine what the scene would be even for a few hundred humans who were without water for two or three days. And for several thousand, some of whom are actually dying of thirst, it would be a nightmare of humans turned into worse than frenzied animals.

I know that water for the millions, is no doubt the responsibility of governments around the world. But I insist that due to the need, the future need and the waste of nature's most valuable liquid, not enough has been done anywhere to alert the pupulace to recognize the great wealth we have in pure water.

Over the past 15 years I have searched and checked in this district of Loudoun County, for a waterfall, or a big spring, that rises high up in the mountains and bubbles out of rocks and gravel and falls down the mountain. I have not spent all of my awake hours in the quest but to date, along the Blue Ridge Mts. and other lower ranges, I have been unable, in the time I have had, to locate such a flow. There are plenty of springs high up and I know there are domes at the highest points, but never a big gushing spring or an actual water fall. Yet over in West Virginia, I understand there are good water falls and also in southern Virginia. I wonder why there are none in the Blue Ridge?

I had a call from Jim Tyler, a local real estate broker. He had a small farm about to be sold but the buyer wished to be sure of a permanent supply of good water before the sale was finalized. There was a good spring and an old stone spring house on the property, which had no doubt supplied water for the whole property over the many years. However the health department would not approve the spring as fit for human consumption, so Jim had persuaded the seller to drill a well. Jim picked me up at my office. It was a nasty day. We had had an ice storm the previous night and the Blue Ridge Mts. were covered with ice. The trees glistened in the morning sun. It was a very beautiful sight, like a glass world, but boy it was cold! We got to the farm and immediately I could see why the health department had turned down the spring. The spring house (as most of them are) was settled in a low spot near the old stone house and a pond. The pond was fed by the spring's overflow, but over the years, the pond had silted up, overgrown with grasses, etc. and had become actually higher than the overflow from the spring house. So instead of the spring flowing into the pond and then on out at the other end it was backing up around the spring house. I mentioned to Jim Tyler, if a mechanical blade was used to clean out the pond and run-off beyond, it would again become an excellent spring and water source. But he said, as it had already been turned down by the

66

health department it would be cheaper to drill a new well for immediate use and, at a later date, the pond could be cleared and the spring house used again. So I scanned the area and found two sites close by, in the ice covered, 3 feet high, grass and vegetation. The maximum depth was 200 feet at 8 gallons per minute. After marking the site with a wooden stake and red ribbon, we hurried back into his car. I was cold even though I was dressed for the occasion, with rubber hunting boots, thick socks, long johns, blue jeans and a fur lined short coat. Jim must have been frozen, as he only had on a business suit, low shoes and felt hat. I noticed his nose was almost blue. I think his car was a big Lincoln and, as soon as the motor started, it became nice and warm and we got comfortable quickly as we drove away.

After leaving the back roads, we hit the main highway and we were headed through a cut with high banks on either side. Suddenly up ahead we saw two or three cars stopped. A panel van was upside-down at the right hand side of the road. A small sedan was in the middle of the road, with no front-half visible anywhere. There were several people laid out on the grass verge, being attended to by others. Jim and I said it looked like a nasty head on accident. He at once picked up his citizen band mike and reported the accident. The steam was still rising from the car in the middle of the road, so it must have happened minutes before we arrived.

At that time, we saw a black puppy with a white cloth leash trailing. He was running along the right hand side and headed up the hill. Jim said, "We can't let that poor little fella get up into those woods. He would not survive the night." I agreed and we both jumped out and ran up the high bank after him. The highway wire fence stopped him from going on through and we grabbed him. He was all covered with anti-freeze, in shock and his little heart was pounding like a drum. It was evident he had been in the accident. There was nothing we could do further, so we drove on. I had the pup on my lap and as we passed the overturned vehicle, we told a chap who was helping that we had the pup and who we were.

There was a trace of blood on the pup, so when we got to my office, we took him inside and examined him. We found no cuts, just a couple of lumps here and there. We decided that I should take him home for the night. I had noticed the big bones, big pads and strong head of the pup. I told Jim I thought he was part Newfoundland or Labrador breed. He could not have been more than 3 months old. My wife, Barbara, and I have had animals around us all our lives. At this time we had none, but as we are getting older we had no intention of having any more. We believe and know that it takes time, love and patience to do justice and properly care for an animal and one must be active with them. We have all of these except the activity, so we decided against keeping the pup. We soon had him comfortable. He drank and ate a little and we were very surprised at his understanding and obediance. When told to sit, he did so at once; when told to lie down, he obeyed immediately and when told to come, he came at once. I took some pictures of him carrying my slipper for me. We did not know to whom he belonged so we informed the police and the dog warden that we had him. The next day the dog warden, a young lady, came and collected him, saying they would check to find out if someone in the accident owned him. About a month later, we got a call from a young lady, thanking us for rescuing him. She said she had been in the upside-down panel van and had been taken to the hospital and her big worry, while in the hospital, was her pup. She had just gotten out of the hospital and was feeling much better. Now that she had her pup back she was feeling great. Her father had gotten him for her. He was about 3 months old and was a Newfoundland/German Shepherd cross. We told her we loved him and would liked to have kept him but, at our age, we had decided against any more pets. It just shows that water dowsing can lead one down many paths. I omitted to say that two elderly people were killed in that nasty accident. Also later the well was drilled and came in as foretold making the seller, buyer and of course, Jim Tyler very happy.

I am not able to relate at length any authentic instances of dowsing that occurred far back in history, other than that which is written and described by scholars and historians, who are much more learned than I and able to put such facts before the reader, as in the writings of Kenneth Roberts, where the detail of dowsing practices opens the minds of all who are interested. Therefore I dare not trespass into this realm of scholarly wisdom, but must stay with the simple facts and truths I have encountered personally. I must say I have gained great benefits and improved my practices and results, from reading and using the advise written by such gentlemen and ladies.

I will take the liberty of relating an article written by Bruce Kakaroff, in the magazine "Petroleum Today" written in 1973, and entitled "Science, Superstition and the Search for Oil." "Today's oil and gas hunters are aided by such complex scientific instruments as the seismograph, the magnetometer and the gravimeter, but throughout the petroleum industry's history, there have always been some who began a search for oil by consulting a ouija board, a crystal ball, a divining rod or the promptings of E.S.P."

In the late 1950's, an oil company was carrying on an intensive program in southern Michigan, using all the scientific tools and techniques available for such an undertaking. One farmer refused to lease his land for exploration. Instead, he consulted a fortune teller who told him exactly where he would find oil . The farmer drilled a well for himself, according to her instructions. The oil company's scientific team was still evaluating the data from it's geological and geophysical efforts when the farmer's wildcat well came in as an important discovery.

It is reported that the company's production superintendent said, jokingly of course, "Fire our geologist and hire that fortune teller." It is easy enough to scoff at superstition as a factor in the hunt for oil, yet most skeptics, who spend any time in the production end of the business, sooner or later have chastening experiences.

Long before geologist were used in the oil industry, the talents of water dowsers were frequently employed, using dowsing rods or doodlebugs, which were often just "Y" shaped tree branches, to detect the presence of water or oil. They were such fixtures in the industry's early years that today's oil people call the seismograph a "doodlebug." Many years ago, a Texas rancher who leased some of his land for petroleum exploration, had dabbled with dowsing, before drilling began. He went over part of his property with a dowsing rod. He drove a stake in the ground at a spot where the witching wand had indicated the presence of oil. Soon afterwards the drilling crew came along, but no one was around to tell them where the well was to be drilled. So when the men saw the stake, they assumed it was the marker for the drilling site. They drilled down more than a thousand feet before someone realized a mistake had been made. By that time it was too late to stop , so they kept on drilling and found oil. After that a well was drilled on the site that the oil company had actually chosen. You guessed it, that well was a dry hole.

CHAPTER 9

POWER BEYOND BELIEF

I read of an elderly farmer up in Pennsylvania who used a large pair of pliers instead of the old traditional forked branch and he had great success. So I tried this out and I was very surprised at the amazing results. I have used wire from coat hangers, metal rods and have even tried out a couple of plastic rods fastened together. But I always go back to the wooden "Y" branch.

The first time I tried out a big pair of pliers, I was unprepared for the violence of the downward pull as I came over the underground vein. I did as I usually do with my maple rod. I gripped very tightly with the intention of holding until I could hold no longer. Well the pliers, which had short legs to hold on to and no whip or flexibility, went down quickly and at once. As I gripped harder to try to hold them, I was brought up onto my toes. The pliers dug into my hands with such force and pain, I had to let go. I do not use this plier method, but I have had some very comical times demonstrating with the pliers to other people. It certainly is a very persuasive manner to show skeptics the power of the rod. I was at Hamiltion, fifteen minutes west of Leesburg, finding a site for a new house which was on 5 acres. Two or three people met me and I went to work. After finding and marking the well site, the observers, as is often the case, wanted to try the rod. There were many of the usual questions and as we were practicing, a neighbor came by, who evidently was an electrician. He made several jokes about our funny games, but he would not try the rod. I talked with him for a minute or two and everyone around was laughing at him for being scared to try. Stuck in his back pocket was a big pair of pliers and I told him he could feel a great force with the pliers if he tried. After showing him how to hold the legs of the pliers, I faced him toward the underground vein and told him to walk ahead slowly, which he did. Everyone was watching him closely. Suddenly he said,

"Lord" and his shoulder hunched up. He went up on his toes and dropped the pliers. He looked around at all of us and, with amazement still on his face, picked up his pliers and walked away. I've never heard from him since.

For those for whom the rod will work, you will find that an enormous surge of power will not allow you to hold a pair of pliers for more than a few seconds after they begin to move downward. I use the type that can be adjusted, large or small, by the adjustment holes in the head of the pliers. By having them in the large position one can more easily hold the legs correctly.

It really is very profound indeed, how the power manifests itself through a pair of pliers. Of course there are, no doubt, other things that can be utilized in place of pliers, but I have not used or tried to find any of them. I know of this amazing strength of the rod, or whatever it is that causes this powerful movement and I believe in it enough to know that it works and is impossible to stop.

We have heard of the great mammoths, being found frozen in ice up in the Arctic Circle, with vegetation still hanging from their mouths, as though, when at the time they were quickly frozen, they were in the act of eating normally. What magnificent power did this? There are many more mysterious evidences of nature's power throughout history, that we take for granted as having happened and could happen again.

Why is it so unbelievable that the ancient art of dowsing can be performed by Henry Gross, Miss Penrose and other talented water dowsers with true prediction, with a forked branch, indicating the exact spot, the depth and quantity of good pure water, which can be found in an underground source?

Here is something that is fact, but cannot be explained. I had an aunt, my mother's sister, who was an herbalist, a minor author and spiritualist. Aunt Meg was a very unusual person, almost stone deaf and everybody loved her. She was quiet, unassuming and dignified. In the company of the family and others, you would suddenly feel she was, and had

72

been, watching you for some time. When you turned and met her eyes, she would smile at you, giving you the uneasy feeling that she saw something in you, or about you, that you did not know yourself.

As a young man, I had returned home from Canada at the time of the 1930 depression. A young partner and I had lost everything in our first start in the logging business. We finally had to give away our two teams of horses, wagons, sleighs and other equipment. It was 1932 when I arrived home in County Durham, England. My father said, "We all come back to the home workshop eventually, but never mind lad, the best steel must go through the fire." So we were visiting relatives, grandmothers, aunts etc., in Darlington and, as we sat around and talked, I felt Aunt Meg's influence. I turned to her and met her smile. She motioned for me to come over to her and unexpectedly she said, "I can see great activity around you and some turmoil ahead of you. But be certain of this, you will go back across the Atlantic Ocean." At that particular moment I had no thought, whatever, of returning to the American Continent. However after the Second World War ended, which of course was 5 1/2 years of turmoil, I returned to America in 1952. In 1936 I had met my wife-to-be, Barbara Jane. Again we visited the North Country and met Aunt Meg again. After we had left, Barbara told me, "Your Aunt Meg had a long conversation with me and she said we would be married and we would lose 3 children, but we would eventually have one daughter." We were married in 1938 during the war years. We lost 3 children and in 1953 we had a daughter, born in Sharon, Connecticut. She is our only living child. She is now 28 and happily married. Aunt Meg passed away at the age of 86. During her lifetime, she has told many people facts about themselves, that they alone knew, or things that would happen to them which came true with astonishing accuracy.

What is this power given to a selected few? There is no accounting for this power. It has never been explained, yet it is a fact that it does exist.

I do not associate the power of the dowsing

rod with Aunt Meg's power of mind or her great
ability to foresee the future. But there must be like
powers, or the same power in different forms, that
we are unaware of that only need development.

It is said that there are electrical forces
within the human body, in large or small amounts. I
have an abundance of this electricity. I cannot open
a metal door without a shock to my fingers. My wife
will not allow me to touch her quickly because of the
sharp shock. When removing my clothes at night,
sometimes little blue sparks will fly. I can take off
my shirt, hold it up in one hand, keeping the other
hand about 4" to 5" away and while moving the shirt
up and down, I can make it rise and fall or turn and
flow in any direction. Once while flying across the
Atlantic at perhaps 35,000 feet, I was in the
passageway and an air-hostess wished to pass. I stood
to one side and as she was beside me, there was a
slight movement of the plane. As I put out my hand
to steady her, I touched her shoulder. Whereupon
there was an inch long blue flash from my fingertips
to her shoulder, which made her recoil from the
shock and the audible snap of the spark. I understand
this is considered to be static electricity, but why so
much more in one person than another?

With the pendulum, there seems to be at times
the indication of an electrical current and sometimes,
when I use the two angle rods and they cross and
touch each other, I can feel a slight magnetic feeling
as though they would stick together.

With the wooden dowsing rod, I do not feel
any type of electricity, just the strength of the pull.
It was according to the actual feel of the pull that,
in the beginning, I estimated or guessed at quantity.
When I was over a vein of water, I could easily tell
the direction of flow by the extra strong pull down
stream as it were. I feel there must be some relation
to electrical vibrations and the width of an
underground stream, as I related previously in using
180 degrees of a circle, starting at the outer edge
and walking toward the center. I get the first pull,
whereupon I stop and mark the spot, then go on to
the center. Again, as stated before, this distance

74

from the first pull to the center, is the same in each half. This does not mean, that this is the actual width of the underground stream, but it gives me an indication of the outer vibrations eminating from such a stream, as shown in the following sketch:

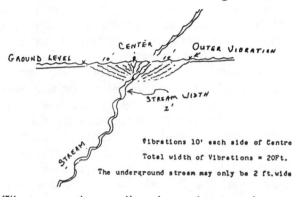

Vibrations 10' each side of Centre
Total width of Vibrations = 20Ft.
The underground stream may only be 2 ft.wide

What are these vibrations that angle up and outward to the surface? Are they electrical? They evidently come from the water, which is flowing. It has been said by other dowsers, that this width of vibration gives them depth. I cannot see that this is true (at least not in this area) as I have found that I could have the width of vibration to be total of 30 feet, and yet the first indication of water is at 130 feet down. So I do not understand the significance as yet, of these vibrations. They are certainly strong enough to halt one's forward movement to the center and yet, when I stop at the first sign of such and stand still and hold up my rod again, the rod does not move. But as surely as I begin again to move forward, the rod can be felt coming to life again. This I do not understand, and again the actual center pull strength is so much more than the first outer pull. Perhaps I am now trying to fathom the exact cause and reason for the rod's behavior, when I have already stated I do not know why it works and that greater minds than mine have already said the same thing. So I'd better just think about it and not ask why. But it is very provoking. No doubt as more people begin to believe dowsing and it is accepted for it's practical ability, answers to many questions will come to light.

CHAPTER 10

LANG MAY YER'R LUM REEK"

I have delayed for too long in joining the American Society of Dowsers, and have just recently applied for membership. I must admit being tardy in answering some very nice letters I have received over the years, from Harvey Howells, Terry Ross and others. I must make an effort and write these fellows. P.B. Smithett, (Secretary British Society of Dowsers) wrote me a nice letter and sent some literature. I remember an article by Edwin Taylor, Esq. of Northumberland and County Durham, my home area. I had occasion to visit his farm and see some of his grand cattle. I notice that he is now a member of the Council of the British Society of Dowsers. Terry Ross made mention in his letter to me, that I might find, that in the future, a device might not be necessary for location, depth, flow and quality. There are classes, he said, for deviceless dowsing and one will know when one is ready to throw away the stick and the answers begin to come to you before you get the reaction. Now this is "far out" to me. I do not disbelieve, I just don't know and until I do, I shall hang on to my rod.

Again tonight, on the news, great concern was expressed for the water shortage across the U.S.A. Weathermen see no substantial rainfall for at least six months, which would make 1981 a very dry year. We, here in this northern neck of Virginia, have had no rainfall of any consequence for the past six months and people are warned not to wash cars or water lawns, under the penalty of a fine. One town in Connecticut is so short of water, they expect to be supplied by water trucks if no immediate rain is forthcoming. Many businesses are drilling their own wells. On last night's TV weather forecast they showed a map of the U.S.A., with the drought areas colored in brown. Two thirds of the country is suffering from the water shortage. It was said that the St. Lawrence River, the Mississippi River, the Hudson River and the Potomac River are far below normal for this time of year. With the ground frozen, any rain we get will (until the thaw comes) just run off the surface. The same applies to snow. It cannot soak into the ground so the water runs off.

This is February 6, 1981 and this is the longest period I have known, without rain, in the past 16 years. Since August of last year we have had less than one third of the rain we usually get in this time period. If the weathermen are correct about the next six months being dry, we are headed into a very serious water problem, especially for crops.

With all this shortage in reservoirs and rivers and the drought of the last six months, I have been called upon to select about 12 new well sites, all of which have produced amply and not fallen off in their supply. I was told today that a small township near here will be calling me soon to locate another well site for them as their impounded supply is running low.

Evidently when there is plenty of water, the skeptics are abundant, but when a serious shortage occurs the number of skeptics decreases. What does a city do when it's reservoirs run dry? Scientist, geologists and engineers cannot tell when the next earthquake will occur, as stated by other writers. They cannot select sites for oil wells more accurately than one in ten. I wonder if they could select well sites for water. Perhaps they can. I am merely wondering what the situation might be.

Please understand I am not making light of the subject. It is much more serious than the general public knows and the long term consequences take their toll also. Should the present drought become worse, I hope that the officials in all jurisdictions will be aided by science and engineers to plan ahead for the water that will be needed for the future's increasing population.

In the meantime, I expect to continue to find water and well sites for those who live outside the cities and towns and must have their own water supplies.

An associate of mine told me he had just had his oil tank filled and he said, "Guess how much per gallon?" I knew it was about $1.05 last month, so I said, "Oh, about $1.15." He told me it was $1.35. We said that in many parts of the country it is much higher than that. He remarked, that if the water situation gets worse, he will bottle the water from his spring to pay for the oil costs. We were just joking, but it is entirely possible that good water could equal the price of gasoline or oil. If, some years ago, someone had made a car engine to run on water, it would already be at $1.35 a gallon. But as far as the general public is concerned it is FREE. I venture to forecast that even without a drought and shortage, the day is not far off when the cost per gallon of water running through city and town water meters, to each individual home, will skyrocket in price. The people with their own good wells on their property, will thank their lucky stars and the dowser who found it for them. Edgar Cayce said the day would come when the man on the side of a mountain with good grass and a spring of pure water will be the millionaire of tomorrow. This I stated toward the beginning of this writing.

Assuming that there are great volumes of water within the bowels of the earth and that, during drought periods, when reservoirs and public supplies are low, one can still drill down and find good water and that existing wells have dropped very little, still supplying excellent flow's of water, would it not be a good idea to have a back-up system of local wells on which to fall back?

As a boy, some 60 years ago, in the Northumberland District of England, I remember at different places along the roads, pipes came out of stone walls, evidently fed by springs above. Each had a flow of water falling into a big stone trough. Some times there was an iron cup attached to a chain, for people to use to get drinks. Horses also drank at the trough. In many villages there was the village well, with a big stone trough and a large handled manual pump, where passers-by and livestock could drink. I feel that as sub-divisions are built and attached to town sewers and water, the local authorities should make it mandatory that the developer should be required to drill a well for every 50 homes, in a central position when possible. Several responsible residents would hold a key, as the pump (hand pump that is) would be kept locked when not in use. The well and pump might be constructed to look like the old village pump and trough, as follows: Square, round or oblong: stone, brick or frame to correspond with the locality.

Then in times of shortage, or long electrical cuts, the village pump could be utilized. Fifty homes would be about 150 people, like a small hamlet, with it's own emergency supply of good water. I would say that the total cost would not exceed $5,000.00 for the finished job, (well with big pump, stone or brick trough, upper structure and roof, etc). This would be $100.00 per unit or residence or $33.33 per person, which is a small price to pay for water in an emergency. There would, of course, be more stringent health department requirements than they had 60 years ago, but a small committee of the 150 residents, could be responsible. The unit's upkeep and hygenic use and it's operation, perhaps once a month, would not take much effort. The area chosen for the site could be a very nicely landscaped and attractive spot, with an interesting seat or bench, like a little park area.

My poor sketch is just a suggestion. It could be designed in many different styles, but the simpler the better, like the big, old pumps used to be. My home is an old type frame colonial. It is older than I. We have our own well and separate hand pump. If I was to build a new home, I would certainly have a separate well with it's own manual pump. In this area, in mid-winter of 1966, there was no water shortage and everything was fine, when suddenly we had a nasty blizzard with heavy snow and howling winds for days. Most of the all-electric subdivisions within the town are dependent on town water. But the 3 to 10 acre subdivisions outside the town limits have their own septic systems and wells. Most of these have electrical submersable pumps sealed into their wells. Practically all the houses have fireplaces and the people could keep warm even if only in one room and they could cook and heat food and liquids on their open fires. But they had NO WATER. The roads were impassable, no way in or out, and army helicopters had to drop baby foods, milk and water in to them. All electric power was out for days. If these subdivisions had had their own community wells, they could have managed very well. The non-existance of basic water caused great problems, regardless of having everything else they needed. Water was their main concern.

I just spoke to a friend, James Harrison Monroe. I just call him "Jim" but, between you and me, I think he likes to be called Harrison. He might well be proud of his name, as he is a descendant of President Monroe. But more important, I think, he is Chief of the Monroe Clan of Scottish fame, here in the U.S.A. Upon bidding him goodnight, I quoted "Lang May Yer'r Lum Reek" (Long may your chimney smoke). This is an old saying, greeting or farewell from Scotland, which, I believe originated in the small hill farms of Scotland. The people there were crofters, generally living some distance apart. As long as each neighbor could see smoke coming from another crofter's cottage, or each of their farm cottages, they knew all was well with the others. But if it was noticed that no smoke was coming from a particular chimney, it was a signal that something must be wrong at the abode and the neighbors would gather to go and see if assistance was needed. As long as the chimneys smoked or reeked it was considered "all was well", hence, the saying, "LANG

MAY YER'R LUM REEK." After I had said it and left the phone, my mind went back to Scotland, the Border-Country and the British Isles and I began to consider their water supplies for almost 70,000,000 people. The British Isles could fit inside many of the states here in the U.S.A. I wonder what the governor of New York State would think if he had 70,000,000 people within his state. If you look at a world atlas, you can see that the whole of the British Isles can almost be squeezed into any of 30 of the states.

At 100 gallons of water per person, per day, for 70,000,000 people, this would be 7,000,000,000 gallons per day needed for humans. Then there would be water needed for industry, livestock, hospitals, public use, etc. I will find out just how much water Great Britain uses per day. She must have used an awful lot of water over the centuries. Does all this come from the sky as rain? I know the British Isles have a heavy annual rainfall. There are answers which I mean to find out.

I had a call from the National Children's Rehabilitation Center. It seems that Tom Hatcher told their business manager, Kermit C. Zieg, to check with me regarding a new well site. They have one well which produces 6 gallons per minute and the water is pumped up into a tank on a tower. This water is to supply all their needs. The average population of the center is 80 persons per day and at 100 gallons per person, they use 8,000 gallons of water per day just for humans. Considering what is needed for lawns, gardens, boilers, and pools, the 8,640 gallons produced by the well is not enough and the Center is still expanding. They will need, at least 30,000 gallons per day in the future. I met with Col. Zieg, who explained all of this to me. He was kind enough to supply me with a partial survey plat of the area and buildings and also an aerial photograph. Well, this is a test for me now and we shall see what my map dowsing can accomplish.

I have already established that there are 5 underground veins on the property, two of them join, and there is a spring rising from one of them at the highest point above the buildings. I have depths of from 160 feet to 220 feet and gallonage from 6 gallons per minute to 25 gallons per minute and all the veins produce good potable water.

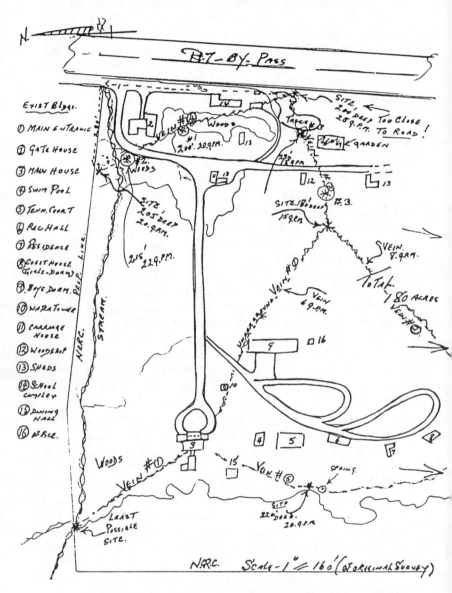

The above is a rough copy of the original plat, with veins marked with dots and dashes. I have marked four possible sites. Now I must go on the land

and check out the sites and see which one will be most convenient for their purpose, considering of course, distances to present pump house and storage tanks and the maximum flow that can be obtained. As I will not get on this land for some days, I will come back again to this project and give the actual facts and final results later in this writing.

CHAPTER 11

WHERE DOES IT COME FROM?

Lucas Phillips told James Lucier about me and my dowsing. Mr. Lucier was about to build a new house approximately 6 miles north of Leesburg. When he came to see me, he had already started building on his 12 acre tract. The driveway was off Route 15 and was fairly level. I would say it was about 1,000 feet long to the house, which was being constructed on the north side, or right hand side as I drove in. On the south side of the driveway, opposite the house, the ground rose to a hillock perhaps 30 feet above the drive level. Jim Lucier wanted to have the well site on the knob about 150 yards from the house. So in scanning the surrounding area, I found that a vein did break out from the hillock and run toward the house and, in following it's course, I found that within 25 feet of the house, the pull was very strong. (This was some years ago, before I could calculate depth and gallonage properly). I figured the flow was twice as strong at this spot than it was up the little hill. So I marked this site and told Jim it was a very strong pull and that it was probably less than 100 feet down. He still wanted the well to be on that little hill, but he finally decided to take my advice and also save the cost of trench, pipe, cable, etc. Some time later he came to my office, gave me a check and said, "Do come when you can and we will have a drink of Scotch, with some of your good cold water in it." I asked, "Did you get a good flow?" He said, "Flow! It's almost artesian. We got 100 gallons per minute and it ran over the top of the casing and did not settle below the top for several days." They had drilled down to 90 plus feet when the water came in, so they went on to 110 feet and quit.

Just south of me about 1 1/2 miles, on the east side of Route 15, a Mr. Jewel had built a very nice brick house. He had drilled to 500 feet and only got about 1 gallon per minute. Next to him was an acre of ground that his son, Don Jewel, acquired and began to build a similar brick house. He called me one night and asked if I would dowse a well site for him. As always, I went and in front of his already started foundation was a big heap of top soil and earth, excavated for the basement. I scanned around and found a vein that ran across the front of his house, right underneath the big pile of earth. It continued on, onto his father's land and ran under the rear corner of his father's house. After checking it out and marking the site so it did not interfere with his driveway, I used Bishop's Rule and paced off 52 yards, or 156 feet. From that spot I paced on for another 30 yards before the rod moved. Then it went down strongly. I was uncertain about the 90 gallons per minute flow. I did not feel sure about it and after re-checking two or three times, I found that I got a quick pull of the rod at 20 yards and then the strong pull at 30 yards. So I told Don Jewel, "156 feet deep and a flow of 60 gallons per minute." One day, later, he called me, then came to my office, smiling and happy. He said his father's face was green with envy. They got more than 100 gallons per minute at 160 feet and the water is steady at 9 feet from ground level in the casing. A friend of mine said, "That's what makes a house a home."

Tom Hatcher says he won't have a well drilled, for himself or clients for whom he does all the plumbing and fitting of pumps etc, until he calls me to mark a site. This is all very gratifying, but it also makes me feel very responsible. As I wrote previously, Tom Hatcher observed Henry Gross at work and realized he was watching a master. It would not be possible for me to achieve such status. I am very glad to be able to help and also am pleased with my progress, but I have a very long way to go. At present I am very satisfied and gratified to be able to help those who are in need of water.

Tom Hatcher took me with him to a 200 acre farm, where most of the acreage was in pasture and there was a good sized herd of steers grazing. One section had a large cattle trough in a fence line, so that cattle could drink from either side in separate pastures. A small pump house was also situated above a well in line with the dividing fence. The water, however, had become muddy and thick, so they had Buck Lawson come and drill deeper at the same spot, but with no luck. The underground vein had become a muddy soup and it was decided they must find a new site. This did not please the owner. He did not want the expense of new lines and re-establishing the pump and house to keep this same trough full. However when Buck Lawson tried to retrieve the steel casing they had already sunk, his rig could not pull the casing up. The suction below overcame the lifting apparatus and, when they let the casing go, it just sucked back down and out of sight. This convinced the owner that his well had turned into a sink hole. So Tom and I headed uphill for firmer ground which again caused the owner to complain about the distance we were going away from the old site, and the cost to him. It was necessary to tell him that water is where you find it, not where you want it.

Finally about 200 yards and 50 feet higher up the hill, I found and marked a grand site. The vein was coming from a wooded area about a quarter of a mile up the slope and headed directly for the original old well, down in the low spot near the tank and trough. I estimated, and told Tom Hatcher, that the vein was at 150 feet deep and would flow at 75 gallons per minute and then I left.

Some time later, I met the owner in town. He came over, shook my hand and said how appreciative he was and what a wonderful flow of water he had. The abundance had evidently overcome the eventual cost.

About 8 miles north of us here, along the Virginia side of the Potomac River, there is a red, rocky, cliff-like wall that rises about 250 feet straight up from the edge of the river. Many years ago an owner of the property above had built a home of this red rock and heavy timber. There was a walled promenade across the front overlooking the river. It was a beautiful spot. You could see up and down the river and across to Maryland for miles and you could cast a fishing line well out into the river.

There are some nice bass along that stretch of water. The house was very well constructed from this red rock and big roof timbers, and originally , it had been beautifully landscaped. There was also a good sized swimming pool and bath houses. The old spring, back in the woods, must have been a good one, supplying the premises, by means of an iron pipe, with plenty of good water. But the spring had gone dry and, as it was on someone else's land, an easement was required. The new owner wished to find a well site on his property but he only had about 3 acres of wooded area right on top of his solid red rock.

I was asked to go and check, and when I got there and looked around I thought, "Not much chance here, solid rock all around." Anyway I began to scan the tract and, by golly, smack in the middle of the tract, among a bunch of scrub trees and briars, I found a site, 100 feet deep and a flow of 8 gallons per minute. They drilled and put in new pumps and tanks, etc. That was, perhaps, 6 years ago and they've had no trouble since. The name of the place is well known around here. It is "Red Rock."

Earlier, I mentioned a well site at a quarry and crushed stone company. It was at that time that I tried my first long distance dowsing. As I said, I knew that they had started drilling, but I did not know the final results. Upon phoning the owner I found that his remarks and answers confirmed my long distance queries to my rod, and today I received a very nice letter from the owner. It has been 6 weeks since I dowsed the well site, about four weeks since I did the long distance dowsing and about 3 weeks since I called by phone to ask the results. His letter has given me proof which I needed, and I find from his letter (see page 57) that they had drilled two wells previously, put in their tower and tank and got only 1 gallon per minute.

This brings me back again to the question of underground bodies of water. I am more convinced than ever now, that there must be enormous bodies of good, clean, pure water, within the bowels of the earth. The article by Bill Broadley, "Dowsing and

•

87

Hydrogeology on Cape Cod" in the February, 1981 issue of "The American Dowser", is an excellent piece of work. I am conversant with many of the terms, but as I am of a simple mind, modern technology leaves me a little cold. I did understand the broad picture, and venture to say, that from a basis of ordinary common sense, it will be shown in the future that those moving channels and vast quantities of water within our earth are independent sources that have always been there. I would ask the following questions:

(1)   After a six month drought, over a large area which was underlaid with solid rock, even a 1 gallon per minute well continued to supply water. From where did this water come?

(2)   On a small rock island, under a blistering sun and under drought conditions for 9 months, a well is drilled below sea level and it produces 15 gallons per minute. From where did this water come?

(3)   A small oasis in the desert has a cool well, producing good water for hundreds of years, the nearest oasis and water is 50 miles away, no rainfall for at least 12 months and that which might have fallen is soaked up at once by the top 2 feet of sand. From where does the water for a permanent oasis come?

(4)   At the highest point in the Blue Ridge Mts., after and during a severe drought, a spring breaks out of the rock terrain, cool and sweet. Before it trickles a few hundred yards the thirsty ground licks it up. From where does it's source come?

Many similar questions could be asked and probably will be asked along the same lines. I know the rod works, but I do not know why. I also know that during the most severe drought conditions, a well site can be drilled to produce water from within the earth. But again I don't know why, I only know it is there.

A volcano, I understand, is a conical hill of erupted materials, which come from within the bowels of the earth.

A dome is a round or polygonal roof. A dome of water must then rise from deep down, due to pressures, and is generally found at different elevations but more often on the higher ground. As I have previously mentioned, rivers do not run up into the mountains. Where there is a dome of water on a high rocky prominence, any rainfall that hits that rock point quickly runs downhill and is gone before any great quantity can supply the dome. What causes the great pressure that forces water up through a mountain and from what source? Scientists have been searching for signs of water on Mars, Jupiter and other planets for many years. I understand they are now able to examine strata below the surface of some planets, with the prospect of being able to know of the existance of liquids within these bodies. It would certainly be very exciting if they found that water existed below the surface of some planets, which has no rainfall or moisture in it's outer atmosphere. But perhaps I am being too imaginative and I better stop at this point, though it is very intriguing.

I just had a call from a lady who said she had been advised to call me before she drilled a well. She had 3 wells to drill, as she was selling her main farm house and some land and was going to build two residences on two 10 acre tracts. I asked her what was the present source of her farmhouse water; she told me it was from their wonderful 200 year old spring which had never gone dry and was excellent water. It seems that the buyer would not finalize the sale until a good well was drilled, regardless of the excellence of the spring. She also said, she had called a well driller and he said he could be there within an hour. I told her I could not possibly come immediately, but if the weather was favorable, I would come in two days. She said she would let me know what happened as the well driller had already arrived. So we shall see soon what occurs and I will relate the results later.

89

CHAPTER 12

SOME OF MY BEST FRIENDS ARE DOWSER

I saw Tom Hatcher today; he was in the back room of his plumbing establishment, cleaning some mud off his shoes. Tom is about 80 years old now and he had just been out in the hills checking on a job. When I walked in he said, "Why look at you here. I've not seen you in a coon's age, Dick, how are you? Come on let's go into the office and sit down," which we did. I had not intended staying long, but , by George, I was there for an hour. Tom is the "salt of the earth," old, mellow, wise, kind, a friend and he is just a damn fine gentleman. He has had Parkinson's disease for years. It's an awful job for him to write and he walks very slowly. I suspected today that he has pain due to arthritis.

We sat down in his office and he said, "Over the years, you and I have seen some odd things with people, wells and water."I mentioned that I had been asked, on his recommendation to dowse a well site for the National Children's Rehabilitation Center. "Yes," he said, "they had considered tying into the town water, but I told them, they have all their own facilities on their property; all they need is a good well." Anyway, in all probability, the cost of town water would no doubt be doubled within a short time and it would be best to have their own water and be independent. I told him what I had done; I had map dowsed the plat I had been given and had found 5 veins and felt there was the possibility of 25 gallons per minute and that as soon as the weather was suitable I would let him know. Then he went on to talk about Henry Gross and some of the things he had seen Henry do, especially one thing. They were at the Paxton home and had been checking the flow of water in the underground caverns and the Paxtons asked Henry how far it was to the source of this water. Henry lifted up his rod and, with his eyes closed as though he was praying softly, he said, "Is it 500 feet?" Answer,"No." "Is it 1000 feet?" Answer, "No." "Is it 2000 feet?" Answer, "No." The rod was quite still each time. Then "Is it 3000 feet?" The rod dipped down, "Yes." Tom said they had previously measured the distance to what is known as Big Spring. They knew it was exactly 3000 feet.

Then he related a story about a very well-to-do man, who owned a lovely property, high up in the Blue Ridge, who needed a well drilled. He called Tom, who had known him for years and told Tom, "I want this well drilled at the corner of the house next to the chimney." Tom told him, "Before you drill, I want to bring a friend of mine here to dowse a site. Don't go drilling until I do. I would not drill for myself until he had checked the area for me." He was told, "Tom, this is my money and I want that well drilled where I have said." Tom told him, "Alright but don't forget you are the one that said so." A couple of days later he called Tom from his city office and said he had ordered the well driller in and asked if Tom would take care of it. So the driller came and began exactly where the owner had said and every morning the owner called Tom at 6 a.m. on the dot, with the questions, "How is it going? How far down are they?" Tom told him 200 feet; the next day 255 feet and so on each day. Finally they were down 600 feet in rock and had 1/2 gallon per minute when the owner phoned Tom and was told they had found so little water. He said, "I'll be there within an hour" and, true to his word, his little plane landed on a landing strip close by and his first question to Tom was, "Well what are you going to do?" Tom said, "Nothing, you chose this spot, you tell me." Tom told him, "There is only one thing we can do now if you insist on this site. That is to put a large concrete tank underground, fill it from what you have in the well and put a pump and pressure tank in the basement to draw from the tank as needed. There will be about 750 gallons reservoir in the well casing, and, as you only come up here week ends etc., it should be enough for your needs." Tom did all of this, which was very costly. Later, without Tom's knowledge, the owner had two more wells drilled, lower down from the house at 500 and 600 feet. Both were dry dust holes.

Then Tom went on to say to me, "Do you remember going up into that area and finding a site for a man who's spring had gone dry? It was early spring; he only had about an acre of ground. You told me about a big circle on the grass at the rear of the house, where two bucks had locked horns in the snow that winter and fought in a circle, leaving the marks behind." I said, "Oh yes, I recall, we got him 20 gallons per minute at about 160 feet." Tom said "That's right, well that was directly opposite from the property I have just related the story about. When he found out that his neighbor used your services as I had wanted him to do, he just hung his head and walked away."

As I left, Tom said, "I'm glad you came in Dick, you have cheered me up." I had said very little, Tom had done all the talking, but evidently he was lonely. As I left I said, "Tom I'll be in to see you again and we will have another chat." I meant it too. They don't make the "Tom Hatchers" or the "Lucas Phillips" anymore and that is a great shame indeed.

I understand that there are many more younger people taking a serious interest in dowsing, which is good. But up to this point in time, any knowledge gained over the years has come from older people. Almost everyone who used the dowsing rod, when asked how they came to know and use the rod says, "Oh, my grandfather showed me," or "An old chap who lived out in the country showed me." So it has taken many years for the few who used the rod to accomplish success, through practice, patience, reading and acting on the advice and practices of others. Under these conditions dowsing has gradually become better known, but generally the expansion has been among those who live outside the city areas, as out in the country side the need for underground water is and always has been a permanent requirement. Very slowly the towns and cities are becoming more aware of the value of the dowser and his underground finds.

One day in the near future, dowsing could become a recognized profession, like the herblist of old, the wheelwright, the midwife or many of the old professions. I notice that in the USSR dowsing has become part of professional school's courses and the USSR Ministry of Geology has sanctioned a book on dowsing. More than that, it is considered as being suitable in courses of higher education. I read that the Soviet term for dowsing is" biophysical" or "biolocational." They evidently believe in underground bodies of water, considering the great number of wells they are drilling for town and farm use. I wonder when responsible people in science, engineering, geology and government, here in the West, will wake up and open their minds to the great potential of the dowsing rod's power. If they observed only a few of the reputable dowsers, without any scientific gimmicks or absurd testings, they would see the actual results and proofs. At least some of them would be convinced. But perhaps some of the scientist might find that the rod worked for them and they would become addicted and that would never do! The only way for dowsing to be recognized here, it seems, would be if an institute of higher learning would act and produce scientific minds who had taken courses in dowsing or biophysical education. We will no doubt wait until Russian University's have proven for us, what old men knew and taught to their grandsons 200 years ago.

I have just had a report on the well that was drilled on the property at Mt. Gilead, where I tried my first map dowsing. (I also got the worst case of flu I ever had.) Anyway the site we chose was near the house and the rod told me there would be 11 gallons per minute at 150 feet deep, so I told them I was very glad for them with the 15 gallons per minute they had found, but if they had stopped at 150 feet they would have gotten, within a couple of days, the 11 gallons per minute as the veins came back in again. But it's no use trying to explain sometimes; people do not listen and understand.

However, once again, a good well and good water; and I feel good about my first attempt at map dowsing. My second one will come up this week at the National Children's Rehabilitation Center. I will relate the results after I have been out on the land and checked the sites.

Dr. Robert Orr, our family doctor for the past 16 years, is a delighted man today, as well as being a very delightful person. About 3 weeks ago, I gave him Harvey Howells' book "Dowsing for Everyone" to read. Last Sunday I was driving by his house and he was just pulling in. He called, "Have you got one of those sticks with you?" I indicated "Yes", then pulled up by his driveway. I took a couple of young maple rods out of my car and walked around to his back lawn, did a quick scan and he came out of his house. I first had him take one leg of the rod and I took the other. Then I had him circle with me to the right and then to the left; in both directions the rod went down. It was an experience just to see his face. "It went down Dick, how does it do that? Here let me try on my own." Naturally I did this and headed him in the direction of the vein I knew was there in his path. Sure enough the rod moved down strongly over the vein for him. We played around some more and he insisted that I leave one of my rods with him. When I left he was going into his house with the rod, talking to himself.

I had occasion today to visit his offices on another matter and collected my book also. He called one of his nurses and, as she got the book for me, another nurse came into his private office. He told them both, "Do you know this works, Dick came to my place with his stick and he showed me how to use it and I tried it and it works. It goes down at once over water." Both nurses smile and one said "Sure", pointing to the floor, "There's plenty of water down there." Well he was quite indignant, saying, "I am serious about this, nurse, it really does work." As I left I told him, "Sir Robert, as soon as the weather is suitable and you have some time available we will get together and do a little dowsing." His comment was, "I'm looking forward to it."

I can understand exactly how he feels; amazed, mystified, startled and completely intrigued. His life has been one of medicine, new scientific medical wonders and caring for people's ills. But, with all his medical knowledge and professional skills, the young maple forked branch, so very basic and simple, is an eye opener to him. Of course it did work for him at once; he had read Harvey Howells' books and he had an open mind. It's great to be able to show the working of the rod to such as he. I always get a kick our of showing someone how it can work for them. His amazement does not surprise me in the least. After 20 years or so, I am still amazed and honestly quite awed at the future prospects of such power.

I have noticed just recently, that I am becoming more affected by the rod and it's power. As I stated before, when I initially use the rod each time I scan a site, the cords or glands in my neck ache and now I find that this is becoming more pronounced. On occasion I get a slight pain across my chest. When this happens, I just stop for a while, perhaps two or three minutes, until it goes away, then I can proceed comfortably. But it does seem to affect me more now and I am very aware of it. After two or three hours of dowsing, I become very tired at night, and the back of my neck aches as it did thirty years ago after a heavy days work back on the farm. I expect it's age and I just won't recognize it.

This morning I was up on the side of the Blue Ridge Mts. What a very beautiful day it has been; started out about 22 degrees and went up to almost 60 this afternoon. I went to find three well sites at a farm and high up there it was grand to look out across the county and look up at the Blue Ridge. Birds were singing and getting ready for their 1981 courtships, nest building and family raising, as they have done for many thousands of years. A fellow can find an awful lot of peace and tranquility in such a spot. Just over the Blue Ridge Mts. into West Virginia and even the western part of Loudoun County on the eastern side of the Blue Ridge, the view reminds me so very much of the Border Country and Northumberland, the dividing line between England and Scotland. Better not get carried away in sentiment but it's a beautiful world.

CHAPTER 13

LOOKING BACK

This is February 17, 1981 and this morning I listened to "Morning" with Charles Kuralt and Gordon Barnes on television and to their discussion on the drought across the country and the water shortage in general. The whole program could have been taken from the forword of these writings, exactly as I have written it. I am so glad to see such on television. It cannot be stressed too strongly. In fact a campaign should be started NOW and kept on, to impress upon the public the seriousness of the water situation throughout the whole country. I have seen this critical time coming for years, but as usual people have to be hurt before they believe.

Gordon Barnes estimated that even if we had six months rain, it would not be enough to satisfy our ever increasing needs. We have already gone through six months of fall and winter drought and his estimate is that we are in for a dry summer in 1981.

It is a fact that small towns and suburban locations, that five years ago had populations of 10,000 to 15,000, are now swollen to 20,000 and 35,000 and continuing to increase. As I related earlier, every household today needs three bathrooms, washer, dishwasher, sprinkler system, pool and anything else that will use water. A family of five today will use 750 gallons of water daily, whereas back in the 1920's this probably would have been a week's supply. It is very easy to develop new scientific wonders and we all love our gimmicks and modern way of life, but we can't produce good clean water on a production line. Maybe the time has come when dowsers can get together to show the officials the folly of their ways. But what would you expect if you waved a dowsing rod in front of Congress? Probably laughter and ridicule.

Ten years ago we were warned about oil and energy shortages, but nothing was done to prepare for it. Now we are in a big scramble to try to get out of our dependency and to use our own resources. We had to be hurt first. The time is fast approaching when the shortage of water will cause a much more severe hurt.

Gordon Barnes mentioned in his broadcast, that the underground aquifer's (the dictionary definition of aqua is "water", aquiferous is "conducting water" and aquiform is "in the state of water." Therefore, I am led to understand that aquifer is "an underground water-saturated area"),are becoming depleted, meaning, to me, that those areas of underground, water-saturated strata are dependent upon rainfall. He was actually talking about our lack of rainfall.

Going back again to the article of Bill Broadley in the February 1981 issue of "The American Dowser", it would seem we have abundant proof to show that only a small percentage of the annual rainfall finds it's way into these aquifer's, therefore, considering the large capacities of such aquifer estimated by Mr. Broadley, there must be vast sources of water coming from somewhere other than precipitation.

I wish to go back again to previously related points of interest:

1. Tom Hatcher being lowered into the Paxton home well, with the caverns below actually flowing at such a speed so as to carry away a large piece of wood very quickly.

2. In a period of six months drought, high up in the hills, wells are still supplying at their usual rate, while the Potomac River, Goose Creek and lowland reservoirs are getting lower daily.

3. The six domes of water coming from below sea level on the Island of Bermuda found by Henry Gross.

4. The statement by Henry Gross, of an underground river in the Sahara Desert and the odd wells, thousands of years old, at the "few and far between" oases.

5. Drilling through 400 feet of rock during a long drought period and getting 22

gallons per minute.

6.   Again during a drought period, the strong flowing spring rising at 2,000 feet elevation.

These facts must surely point to pressures and forces deep within the bowels of the earth that are completely independent of any atmospheric disturbances. Also that domes of water, large springs and wells at high elevations, with no letup in supply, especially during lowland drought periods, must depend on other sources than rainfall. Perhaps we are nearing the time when some of these assertions will be proven and a new outlook will prevail. After all, the world is no longer flat, parts of the Ark are reputed to exist and we do travel in outer space.

In Harvey Howells' book, "Dowsing for Everyone," he goes on from the forked branch and water, to the pendulum, hand dowsing, dowsing for lost property, dowsing the aura, dowsing for missing persons, and remote dowsing. I seem to stick to dowsing for water. I have tried map dowsing twice and will probably do more of it. Long distance dowsing intrigues me with some success and I have had some recent predictions with dowsing for oil. Having acquired three crude oil samples, which I mentioned before, I have only tried them once; but in my home I have asked my rod about the oil location and, without having any of the crude on the tip of the rod, I get the same answers, for depth and gallonage, that I did when I was on the land close to the actual location. So a friend and I are going to experiment at the location and then some distance away and compare notes. This will give me a witness to the actual working of the rod with depth and quantity. I am writing much of this as I am doing it, so within a couple of days of finding water for someone, except for the first half dozen chapters, I have been relating the "on the job work" so to speak.

I believe I spoke previously of a lady who called me from Round Hill, about fourteen miles west of us here, in the foothills of the Blue Ridge. She wanted three wells dowsed at once, as a driller would be there within the hour. I said I could not get there immediately. Later she called me to say he had not arrived and would not be there for several days so I went yesterday on George Washington's birthday,(his ancestors came from the Border Country; President Jimmy Carter went over to County Durham and visited the little town of Washington). As I wrote,some pages back, the farm house had a beautiful spring about 200 years old, housed in a lovely old spring house. They were selling the house, barns and twenty-odd acres and the buyer had insisted that a new well be drilled. While waiting for the lady owner, I looked over the situation. I could see the general layout and, with the spring house being in a lower area below the house and barns, and the land rising off to one side and behind the house, I felt the best place to start to scan would be up behind the house. But the lady arrived and informed me that a new septic system was also going in and the health department had already indicated the location for the septic field, tanks etc. Naturally they had chosen the high dry ground behind and off to one side of the house and said it would have to be a pumped up system, as this was the only area of satisfactory perculation. They had also indicated where the well site should be, which was in the low area in front of the house, 50 feet from the actual septic tank and 100 feet from the field lines. It did not have to be in any particular spot, but within the range and area they had indicated on the plat. So I went to work near a couple of small apple trees and luckily there was water within the given space, 200 feet down. It was good potable water, 12 gallons per minute and it would come to within 20 feet of ground level. As usual there were a couple of children and a brother watching and they all had to try the rod. I showed each one in turn, the lad first. He was about 12 or 13 years old. The rod worked strongly for him. It did not show much, if anything,for the two adults. But for the little girl, the rod just vibrated and so did the little girls hands and wrists. I fear she was a little frightened but laughed about it afterward.

I did not like the idea of the pumped up septic system being above the well site. I never like to see any well below the level of a septic system. This I told the young lady and her brother. They agreed with me but said they had to abide by the regulations of the health department.

From there we went to a field higher up about one half mile away to a lovely spot that overlooked everything. The young lady had a large survey plat of the whole tract and also health department sketches of where the septic field should go. Again she had a suggestion for the well site. I was able to locate the suggested well site area, because of a small copse near the house that was marked on the plat. But at this particular spot I could only get 6 gallons per minute, at 240 feet. We then moved higher up into the next field, but there was no indication as to where the house was to be constructed. I had to tell them, it was no use going any further with this site, until they knew exactly how and where the house was to be placed. They knew that the septic field was to go in front of the house and the well behind. But, as I pointed out to them, it would not help to have a well drilled in what might be the middle of the dining room. They saw my point and said they would lay out the house, stake it out and call me when it was ready. You know you don't just dowse for people; you advise, you counsel, you explain and you help when you can. Sometimes it is difficult to get through to people and sometimes one can see there is no use even trying. But afterward most people understand and are appreciative.

I wrote about Col. Zieg and the National Children's Rehabilitation Center and I showed a sketch of the property and veins I map dowsed in my home. Col. Zieg called me and said he had to go to Florida and would call me when he got back. Except for seeing the general outlay, and collecting the maps and partial survey plat, I had not been back on the land. He called me this morning and asked if I was available. I said I would meet him at 10:30 a.m. at the gate house. I took along the plats etc. When we met I gave him the plat and showed him my survey of map dowsing, with the veins marked in and each site marked showing the depth and gallonage for each, so that he would know and could see as we moved around, exactly where we were. Naturally he asked many questions regarding my markings on the plat. He could not understand how it was possible for anyone to mark underground veins, well sites, depth, gallonage etc, on a map and then expect to have them correspond to the actual sites found when on the land. However off we went, with him keeping close watch of my direction and the exact spots we found and marked, and also my comments as to what I was doing and why. We started at the gate house and I followed the property line for 280', then turned into the property at a right angle for 40'. This put me on the site of a 1908 stone spring house which I had not noticed on my first visit. This verified my first site. Then we went back to the gate house and the roadway. Again from the property line, I paced off 640' along the front road, where we marked the spot which, again, was true to the map marking. From this point back to the spring house we followed the underground vein which was already marked on the map, across the gate house lawn and, at about midway, I dowsed a #1 site, 200' deep and 20 gallons per minute. We went on to the spring house and I dowsed #2 site, 215' deep and 23 gallons per minute. Then we went back to the area near the garden, below the spot where the two veins came together. There I dowsed #3 site 230' deep and 15 gallons per minute. We now had three sites marked with depth and flow predicted. By this time we had been joined by Frank, the general foreman. Col. Zieg tried his hand with the rod, but to no avail. I think this annoyed him a little. Then Frank tried his hand and the rod obliged perfectly for him. This made the Col. try again and again and finally he did feel a slight movement. Frank was very pleased with his results. I could do no more for them, as they had to decide which one of the sites would be most suitable for the pipe line they had to lay and the size of pumps etc. So I wished them good luck and left them with happy faces.

CHAPTER 14

ALL IT TAKES IS FAITH....AND PERMISSION

It has always been difficult for me to understand why, in my opinion, the natural events of nature are misunderstood, not understood, or have been passed by and in some instances forgotten. New scientific man-made accomplishments have been readily recognized and seized upon (and rightly so of course) but probably to the extent, and in such rapid order, that the everyday things in nature around us, that we take for granted and expect to be with us always at our immediate command, are not considered enough and indeed not studied for their true value.

The statement has been made that the dowsing rod is more widely used by cultured persons than by illiterate ones. But in the days of the ancient ones, I understand the dowsing rod was used by those who were then considered illiterate peasants and indeed were considered not quite sound in mind and actually dangerous people or witches and were sometimes put to death. It was the cultured people of those days, who benefited from the talent of the dowser and yet they were the instrument of his destruction.

It is easy to believe in todays world, and it is becoming more true, that a man is closer to God under a tree on the top of a mountain, than he is in any Cathedral. In such circumstances the faith and trust and belief is very powerful and natural. Nothing can be seen, nothing can be touched, nothing can be heard but there is a feeling, an all enfolding feeling, that has never been explained. A great power is felt and there is an electrifying sensation, especially when there is no disturbance there is a silence around and one's mind is clear and receptive, a spiritual faith that is in all mankind and is part of nature itself.

Through all our lives and all the lives of our ancestors, it has been known that one season follows another; the salmon come in from the sea and fight their way up stream; the Canada geese, the swallows and numerous breeds of birds fly north and south regularly; bears and groundhogs hibernate each winter and bats fly at great speed in the dark with uncanny accuracy. These and thousand of other events occur as regularly as clock work. Many of the courses and routes taken, the actions and episodes, the timing and precision of these animals, birds and fish are exactly the same now as they were for their predecessors and ancestors hundred of years ago. These things we humans take for granted, though we quietly say it's not possible.

We believe there is a sixth sense, an intuition, a guiding power, a faithful response and a natural instinct within and part of these creatures of nature. Why then is it not possible for we humans to have a dormant instinct, a power within us, long forgotten, that on occasion shows itself in such forms as E.S.P., mental telepathy, hypnosis, spiritualism and WATER-DOWSING.

We who are granted the ability, from whatever source, know that we must believe, have faith and accept the fact that we can find water underground in veins and streams. We do not know why this happens, or why the forked branch responds in our hands, any more than todays salmon takes the course inland of it's great, great grandparents at exactly the same time, through the same channels, to the same identical spot hundreds of miles from the sea. We only know it happens. Why then is it so very difficult to believe in a dowser's ability? Without any thought of questioning, the ability of the salmon, animals, birds etc. are accepted because from childhood we were taught that these things are true and we can, if we wish, see for ourselves that these miraculous events do occur.

When I was a boy, there were not many people around except the very old who could or would show the younger generation anything about the dowsing rod. Today there are associations of dowsers and there are classes and seminars. "The American Society of Dowsers" is getting much stronger. "The British Dowsing Association" has been an established organization for many years. Both of these associations were originally formed by men who had broad and open minds, faith in an instinct and, above all, a FEELING which has led slowly but consistently ahead, with a progressive future anticipated. Each dowser today is part of that progression and every time he show's another person, especially a youngster, how to hold the rod and what the result can be, he is speeding the progress begun by the original pioneers. It's a good feeling to transfer your feelings to another and see the belief of such a feeling on another's face, especially when the origin of that feeling stems from nothing but what is good in nature. Who knows, perhaps we might see "DOWSING", the "BIO-PHYSICAL" or the "BIOLOCATIONAL" as part of our university's higher learning, as they are already doing in the Soviet Union.

In 1776, Benjamin Franklin wrote in his "Poor Richard's Almanac":

"WE KNOW NOT WHAT THE WELL IS WORTH
TILL IT IS DRY"

I read that in 1980 the United States used 235 billion gallons of fresh water every day and half of this amount was not replaced by rainfall or snow. Experts say they believe this is the dryest winter since 1883. Also the experts say that the Ogallala Aquifer, covering 160,000 square miles beneath the great plains, is being tapped by wells more and more and some of this underground reservoir is fossil water 25,000 years old. I don't know how deep this massive aquifer is, but 25,000 years is a long time and there must be other large aquifer's here and there across this continent. It may be that they, or some of them, connect and run into one another. If they have been there 25,000 years or more, have they been supplied by rainfall alone? I estimate that for 70 million people in the British Isles at 100 gallons per person per day, they would use 7 billion gallons per day and yet the quote from 1980 U.S.A. daily water use is 235 billion gallons per day for 230 million people. This is 33 times more. Surely there is something wrong with these figures, which means a great deal of research is needed.

I have been thinking about the average amount of rainfall, for the different areas of the world. I don't know what the actual percentages, or figures would be for the different areas, but I imagine they have been fairly constant, with little deviation over many years, except for the great catastrophic changes in climatic conditions caused by nature at odd periods of history. Having made this observation, then one thinks of the requirements of the populations of these different sections of the world, which probably have been geared by circumstances imposed by the amount of rainfall and water alloted to their particular segment of the world, which in turn of course would be dependent upon the actual climate and season for each locality of the world.

Going back 100 years only, the populations of any given areas were much less than they are today and the mode of living was totally different. Therefore the water used and the required rainfall, was much less. I don't think the average amount of rainfall has increased to accommodate the vast increases in populations, the enormous increase in domestic livestock and the massive additional use of water by industry. Therefore if these assumptions are correct, I would think that a decrease in population, or an increase in rainfall is an immediate requirement.

In the same vein, we have become aware of the great world demand for more food, for more energy and for more of everything for the rapidly increasing hordes of humanity. We have not had the least imagination of the consequences or planned for the coming catastrophy if the supply of these things were cut off or drastically reduced. It cannot be repeated too often, the necessity of the most important element, which is WATER.

I am just one person among hundreds who are known, with the talent for dowsing. No doubt there are hundreds more who are unknown. I am at present operating in one small area and I have about 200 wells to my credit, but there are probably thousands of wells that have been drilled in my district that were never dowsed and no exact account has been kept as to the total in any one county alone.

When one thinks of the rapid demand for more and more water, it becomes obvious that there is a vast increase in the number of wells now being drilled, especially in drought periods. So apart from the ever increasing need for rainfall, there is also the ever increasing demand for the underground supply of water in the veins, underground streams and aquifer's. I submit, nature supplies that which she supplies, NOT WHAT WE DEMAND.

There is a lesson I have learned, that may be of help to aspiring dowsers, possibly saving them some of the embarrassment that I encountered at the beginning of my dowsing. It is one thing to locate an underground supply of water for a single famiy home. It is a different situation to locate water for a farm and much more difficult and time consuming to locate an underground source for a township or an industrial complex.

There are small veins and underground supplies that are convenient to a new home being constructed, that are sufficient and permanent enough and can generally be found fairly easily and quickly. Naturally the greater the flow the more pleased the new home owner will be. But as is often the case, wells producing only 1 gallon per minute, 60 gallons per hour and 1,440 gallons per day have kept a household of 6 and 7 people, with visitors on week ends, supplied with no problems for many years. A friend of mine, in too much hurry to wait until I could locate a site for him, went ahead last week and drilled to over 300 feet and only got a half gallon per minute. I understand that at 280+ feet he was becoming very worried since it was costing $8.00 per foot. However, there is just he and his wife, so they will be alright, as I fully expect the flow will go to 1 gallon per minute soon and he will have about a 375 gallon reservoir in the hole.

As the reader can see, a flow of 6 gallons per minute=360 gallons per hour or 8,640 gallons per day and is plenty of water for a small village and could take care of a maximum of 80 people, with the present requirement being 100 gallons per person per day. So it would be safe to have a flow of 2 gallons per minute for the general household.

If you are asked to locate a satisfactory supply for a farm, you will need to know what the requirements are. Is it for a household, water at the barns for livestock, possibly a milking parlor and probably some livestock drinking tanks in the paddocks near the buildings? If so you are looking for, and must locate, a fairly good supply. This might entail more time to locate the source, which might be some distance from the buildings. So one develops a feel of different strengths from the rod as one scans an area. Very often if the farm is an old, well established place, some of the older buildings were built near a spring. Often one can acquire a good supply of water close to the buildings by checking and following the source of the old springs. Of course the greater the supply needed, the more time and patience must be extended to accomplish the goal.

The individual home owner or farmer has a better understanding of what a dowser is attempting to do for him than does the town manager, or the town engineer. They might be steeped in scientific knowledge and might be natural skeptics, due to their background and schooling, whereby many things they do and think come from what they believe to be logical, scientific and proven mathematical facts, which can be seen and readily understood. Generally, I believe this is the case. There are those, in such positions of authority, who have reason to understand and believe, having been assisted and helped by dowsers, when all else failed.

In trying to find substantial amounts of underground water for a town of several thousand people, the dowser is looking for a flow of 200, 300, 400, 500 or 600 gallons per minute. In trying to find this type of source on the actual land, he must spend much time and effort. To accomplish this, the art of map dowsing is a great asset, when he can locate, on a given area on a map, the best and most productive spots for underground water. He can then go direct to these locations on the land and save much time and energy. At these times it is much better that he go alone to verify his findings.

I have had experience with a number of young scientific engineers who went with me but they did not take a serious view of the proceedings. When told there was no significant amount of water in a certain area, they would insist, "Well would you just try here or just over there?" They wanted to have it "this way" or "that way," so they could use their present lines and pumps etc. All the explanation in the world is futile to people who will not listen and all one can do is try to explain and then leave them to learn by their own mistakes, which often happens.

There are certain things which must be recognized. One is that permission must be obtained from a land owner to go onto his land where a dowser has said there is an indication of a good volume of water. Just because a town has had two or three tracts to proceed on, does not mean that water will be found there. First the tract must be found that has an indication of a good supply of underground water. Then the owner's permission must be sought. The aspiring dowser can readily see the great differences between an adequate supply for a young couple in a two bedroom cottage, a supply for several purposes on a farm and the requirements for a town. Bear in mind, you are a hero and a wonderful chap when you supply a new home with abundant water. But your name is mud if you fail to make a town understand why they are the cause of their own failures.

CHAPTER 15

THEY THINK IT'S WITCHCRAFT!

In this chapter, I am entering an article, written by Robin Lind, for the METRO VIRGINIA NEWS, of September 1, 1974, in which I am portrayed. It reads as follows:

"Since recorded history began, the ready availability of fresh water has been the "Sine Qua Non" for civilization anywhere on the earth's surface. Ever since the first creature crawled out of the ocean and began to track the surface of dry land, the search for water has been never ending. Abundant water meant fertile crop yields and the leisure to pursue the quest of knowledge. A scarcity of water meant drought, famine and destruction. Despite man's utter dependency upon fresh water, streams and brooks, springs and wells, perhaps less is known now about where this lifeline comes from than was known before the scientific method gained supremacy over superstition and folklore.

The only known and tried method of successfully locating underground streams of water is called "DOWSING" or "DIVINING" and operates through a process that has yet to be explained. Modern science, because it cannot understand dowsing, has termed it "bunk" and dismissed all the body of evidence which shows that a dowser can indeed find water. The process of dowsing, which involves the use of a forked branch held in both hands pointed away from the body, has been proven many times in Loudoun County. It has also proven unsuccessful, as sceptics will quickly tell you. Dowsing enthusiasts counter with the argument that not all dowsers are equally talented and to discount dowsing on the experience of one bad event, is the same as to deny the belief in all automobiles after once owning an Edsel.

Leesburg real estate agent, Dick Richards, is one supporter of the dowsing method and is, in fact, a dowser himself. 'I've got about 100 wells behind me,' said Richards,'and I have no idea how it works. Since the world began scientists haven't been able to explain this. They think it's witchcraft. Maybe it's electrical impulses in the body, I don't know. I just know it works.'

Richards is regularly called on to dowse properties where water is needed. As recently as August 28th he drove out to the site of Dick Wright's new house south of Leesburg to find a well site. Stepping out of his car, he picked up his dowsing rod, a forked branch he had cut on the property, and held it up in the air, swinging it in a slow arc, he got a "pull" or "feel" in a certain direction and was soon on the spot, his rod dipping uncontrollably pointing at the ground.

'You've got a good vein of water under here,' Richards told Wright, as he walked back and forth until he had ascertained the width and direction of the underground vein. All of this he determined just from the pull on the stick he held in his hands. Stopping and holding his rod upward, he began to walk backward and as he took his thirteenth step the rod dipped again. 'Your water will be 39 feet down,' he said, computing his steps as three feet to the pace and, knowing from experience, his rod will signal him when he reaches a point on the surface which is as far from the pinpointed location of the vein as the water is from the surface. Again he walked back to the center of the location he had picked out and raised his rod. 'Your flow will be about 7 gallons per minute, 'he said, gauging in his mind's eye the downward pull of the rod. When he had finished dowsing, he offered the rod to Wright and showed him how it worked. No luck, the rod remained dead in Wright's hands. Richards tried again himself. The rod nose-dived while he tried his best to restrain it. The bark itself could be seen twisting. 'Now I can't hold that,' he said as he reddened from the exertion. 'That's tearing the hell out of my hands. See?' The palms of his hands showed painful marks where the rod had tried to turn.

The fact that the rod did not move in Wright's hands did not discourage Richards. A common estimate is that only one out of ten people has the particular gift of dowsing and even then many of those are erratic or unreliable.

'Weird things happen to different people,' said Richards. 'One time I was dowsing for a woman and I said, 'Here, try it.' She tried it and the stick kept on turning. She had to move her chin out of the way and it (the rod) turned completely around, twisting the bark off and that's the truth.'

Describing the dowsing rod he used, Richards explained,'You can use anything really. I prefer maple, elm, peach or willow. One old gentleman I knew up in Pennsylvania used a big old pair of pliers. Now take Henry Gross, he was a remarkable man. He was a real magician and he finally had plastic rods custom made, So his hands wouldn't get all torn up,' said Richards. Gross, perhaps the most famous dowser ever, became so proficient and (through the aid of novelist Kenneth Roberts, who wrote and published three books about him) so well known that people from all over the country would ask him for advice. The curious aspect of this advice, however, was that it bore no resemblance to the "Dear Abby" type of advice dispensed today. Gross, when sent a map of a person's property (whether 1 mile or 1,000 miles away) could dowse the map and locate water veins or "domes" (spouts of water rising from the depths of the earth) on property he had never seen before. In addition he was willing to journey to these properties later and pinpoint the exact location of the water. So accurate was he that in late 1949, without having visited Bermuda, Gross dowsed a map of the island and located four domes of water, where for 340 years the inhabitants had believed no fresh water was available. The domes were later located on the ground and drilled, bringing (in 1950) the first fresh water wells ever to be discovered in Bermuda.

Two of Gross' most astounding successes in this country occurred in Loudoun County, one at what is now the Phillips-Nickels Well in Leesburg, the other at Old Oaks, near Virts Corner. 'We had a well that gave about 2 to 3 gallons per minute,'said Col. Frank Mason, owner of Old-Oaks. 'Then it started to give only about 1 gallon every ten minutes. I called my friend Tom Hatcher and said I was looking for water but could get no satisfaction from anyone in Washington. He got me interested in dowsers but they didn't help any. So I got in touch with Roberts and he said to send a map to Henry so that Henry could dowse it by long distance. Well Gross dowsed it from Kennebunkport, Me. and when we drilled we hit water within one foot of where he said we would,' said the smiling Mason. The year was 1954 and the water shortage in Loudoun was acute. From far away Maine, Gross wrote Mason that he had a stream approximately 435 feet wide located at 170 feet from the surface, that extended to a depth of 350 feet. It flowed at 450 gallons per minute. It was the result of the merging of two underground streams nearby, one of which was the same one being tapped by the town of Leesburg Wells and which flowed at the rate of 700 gallons per minute in town. The other stream came from a dome of water which Gross said was northwest of Mason's property. Mason had Gross come down to Loudoun when he had a well drilling rig lined up and the results were almost exactly the same as Gross had predicted. On April 2nd, 1955 water was found at 87 feet and immediately rose to the 45 foot level. Mason continued to drill until he had reached a depth of 181 feet which would take him into the area predicted, by Gross, to be in the underground stream. When tested the water, which was clear and excellent to the taste, proved to be inexhaustible. It was pumped at 33 gallons per minute for 15 minutes and the water level remained at the 35 feet mark without any draw down; then at 55 gallons per minute for three and one half hours without any draw down; and finally at 72 gallons per minute for about an hour until the pump broke down, unable to affect the water level one inch. Quite a change from the previous system which yielded only three quarts per minute at the best of times. 'The only explanation I have for Gross,'explained Col. Mason,'is that he was an unconscious medium. But there it is!'

Former State Delegate Lucas Phillips joined Mason in bringing Gross to Loudoun County and his results are just as startling. Gross predicted that a well could be drilled on a 12 acre tract, owned by Phillips and William Nickels on the north of town near the Paxton home, and produce 650 gallons per minute. The underground stream was, wrote Gross from his home in Maine, over 400 feet in width and extended from 160 feet below the surface to 320 feet below.

An eight inch well, drilled in the summer of 1955 to a depth of 328 feet, proved to be similar to Mason's. Water was struck at 70 feet and the finished well was tested at 300 gallons per minute for a period of 72 hours, with no draw down at all upon the water level at the top of the well shaft. In a proposal from Phillips and Nickels to the town council, to sell the water from the well, it was estimated that it could produce 432,000 gallons per day, enough to supply the entire town's population at that time.

Gross also was informed of the Paxton home well and the caverns at the bottom which had been explored by plumber, Tom Hatcher in the 1930's. He dowsed the area and said a huge stream flowed beneath the Paxton home, flowing at the rate of 1,225 gallons per minute making a turn southward and supplying the Phillips-Nickels Well.

'Gross came down here and said our stream came from up near Waterford,' said Mason. 'He said something else very interesting; we took him up to the mountains and showed him around and he said the countryside was very like Connecticut, but he was surprised by how few brooks and streams there were. Most of the water is underground,' he said.

In Roberts' book "Water Unlimited", published in 1957, Mason is quoted as saying, 'You marked on your map, when you did your long distance dowsing, an area north of Waterford as being the source of Old Oaks water.' When we drove through this section Henry found great activity and a large number of domes.

Gross was also reported to have felt a "checkerboard" effect in the county with areas alive with water and others registering no water.

'Henry Gross was telling me about the stuff and it got so I believed everything he told me; he was so accurate on everything I asked him,' said Tom Hatcher. 'I asked him to ask his ol' stick what direction the water came from that flowed under the Paxton home.(I thought it was an overflow from Big Spring) but he said No, although it came from beyond that direction.'

Whether Dick Richards can maintain his record for accuracy will be determined by Dick Wright, in a matter of weeks,and what all this means for Loudoun County is difficult to explain in concrete terms. Some of the questions that will arise and must be answered, will have a profound impact on the future developement of any area. Why reservoirs need to be considered when underground flows like these exist, should be a matter of concern, not only for environmentalists, but also for watchdogs of the public purse. Another and more perilous consideration deals with the possibility of contamination of these great underground streams. These questions have traditionally been ignored or disregarded in the past because of the inability of scientists to locate these underground systems. The only proof of their existance is in the pull of a small forked branch in the hands of a dowser or water diviner, the practitioner of an art that is the subject of ridicule for all except the THIRSTY."

I feel Robin Lind did a great service with this excellent article.

The well came in for Dick Wright as dowsed at 7 gallons per minute. That was six years ago and the Wright's have no water problems.

114

CHAPTER 16

FROM BONDAGE...TO BONDAGE

I wrote earlier about the lady out at Round Hill who had three wells she wished to have dowsed and drilled. I had gone to the farm property and located two sites for her, telling her I would return and locate the third one when they had the house site laid out. At that time, as I mentioned, I did not like the idea of the selection for the septic system on high ground behind and to the side of the old farm house. With the site for the well on lower ground than the septic systems and in close proximity, is just bad business. However, as you recall I went ahead as requested and located a site. Tonight I got a telephone call from the lady. She was all upset and worried. It seems that due to the required location of pipe lines at the house by the plumbers and builders, the site chosen by the health department for septic tanks and field on the higher ground, could not be utilized. So they had changed the sites completely and now had the septic tanks and field on the lower ground in front of the house, actually covering the well site I had dowsed. Now they said the well site would have to go up on the higher ground behind the house. She said, "Mr. Richards they have done exactly what you felt they should have done and have reversed the sites."

At last she was expecting the well driller to arrive at any time. He was supposed to have been there "within an hour", about three weeks ago. She asked if I could come again and locate another well site. I told her, "As soon as the driller arrives, let him go to the site already marked up on the hill for your first house and then call me. He will be at least a day at that site and that will give me time to come out and locate a new site at the farm house." That satisfied her and she thanked me again and again.

Don't ever take anything for granted, especially health departments and lady farm owners. Perhaps that is a little sarcastic but you see what I mean? One must be dowser, advisor, engineer, diplomat, and counselor all in one, even though you waste your time in some instances.

Oh well, never mind, I will go out there again and get them squared away. I hope they have the third house site marked off, so they will know where the approximate well site should be.

All the houses built in our modern sub-divisions demand two or three bathrooms at least, washer, dishwasher, lawn sprinklers, of course the possible swimming pool and everything else one can think of to use water.

A member of our board of supervisors and I were talking the other day and his great concerns were population increase, taxes, the budget, schools, roads and transport, along with the addition of another 50 thousand souls in the county within the next ten years, doubling the increase of the past ten years. BUT HE NEVER MENTIONED WATER!

No water, no sewers;
No construction, no houses;
No houses, no expansion;
No expansion, no industry;
No industry, no tax base
And so on to stagnation.

It has been said that there is a 200 year old cycle in history, which goes as follows;

FROM BONDAGE TO SPIRITUAL FAITH,
FROM SPIRITUAL FAITH TO FREEDOM,
FROM FREEDOM TO ABUNDANCE.
FROM ABUNDANCE TO SELFISHNESS,
FROM SELFISHNESS TO APATHY,
FROM APATHY TO DEPENDENCY,
FROM DEPENDENCY TO BONDAGE AGAIN.

The foregoing is a picture of circumstances produced by humans, and my purpose in relating these nasty little facts, is to keep reminding the reader of the magnificent value of WATER. It used to be free but today a city dweller's water rate costs increase annually.

Gasoline is about $1.30 per gallon and fuel oil about $1.20. Along with the cost of living, the inflation rate and the interest rates, coupled with the national and the international situation, this becomes the whole "ball of wax" that controls the minds of all people everywhere. Suppose that water was $1.50 per gallon. Then we would quickly alter our attitude and use of water, as we have done with gasoline and oil. Well, be prepared, good spring water is now 90 cents per gallon in super markets. In the old buggy days, good water was like gold and was constantly in the minds of all who lived on the land and raised crops and livestock. The majority of the population today do not even give it a thought.

If you live in an apartment house in the city, think a little about what you would do if the city's reservoirs would go dry and you turn on your taps and nothing comes out. Much more serious than a gasoline or oil shortage, isn't it? Especially way up there in that apartment house. Not a very nice thought, but one that should be seriously considered.

I have been practicing more with the angle rods and on considering the narrations in the postscript of Harvey Howell's book, "Dowsing For Everyone", I have been experimenting with my two angle rods. They are made from a wire coat hanger. I must get a couple of nice copper rods and a pair of plastic sleeves. I think they would be freer to work, unhindered, by my hands. Anyway, I have been able to command the right or left rod, to move individually right or left, or both together.

As I have related we have been in a six month drought and some weeks ago I checked my well, which is 22 feet deep and supplies, normally, 7 gallons per minute, at which flow the water rises to within eleven feet of ground level in the shaft. I found there was only two feet of water in the well and the flow was down to 3 gallons per minute. But this did not concern me in the least, as this same well has supplied this residence and gardens for more than 60 years. During that time a greater number of people were in residence than there are now, when there is just my wife and I. Over that period of 60 years there have been some very severe droughts also.

However we had about 1 1/2 inches of rainfall within two days last week. So last night I took my angle rods and, facing the direction of the well, from inside the house, I asked, "Are there 10 feet of water now in the well shaft?" No movement, meaning "No". "Are there 8 feet of water in the well shaft?" No movement, again "No". 'Are there 4 feet of water in the well shaft?" Both rods came together and crossed in front of me (for me when they cross means "Yes"). So I went further; "Are there 5 feet of water in the well shaft?" Both rods crossed "Yes". So I stopped at that point. I then went to the well, raised the cover and dropped a one inch piece of 1/2 inch pipe, tied to a light line, down into the well casing until I felt it touch water. I marked my line at the top of the well and withdrew my plumb bob. After measuring, I found I had 4 feet 8 inches of water in the bottom of the shaft. I then checked for flow and found that it was running at 4 1/2 gallons per minute.

I know nothing of healing or the laying on of hands, but my wife had been quite ill for a period of two months. Her illness had to do with the after effects of flu on a thyroid and diabetic condition. She was going into the hospital for a series of tests. Without my wife knowing, I asked the rods, "Will her condition, on examination, prove to be of a serious nature?" No movement meaning "No". So I ventured further and asked, "Will the subsequent examination and treatment of Barbara in hospital prove to be good and improve her health?" The rods crossed, "Yes". Boy was I pleased!

I don't know how far this could go, perhaps I am trifling with something beyond my scope. I just don't know what to think or what to say. But I shall keep on carefully with such practice and see where it leads me. I am now asking the rods about wells that have not yet been drilled, at sites that I have already marked and am waiting for the driller. I get the positive answers and the same predictions that I gave at the sites. I have been surprised and astounded by the actions of the forked branch and have gained experience and confidence over the years; so why should I not expect to have similar events to occur with the angle rods?

I am somewhat wary of the awesome power that can cure the human body. It smacks of miracles and miracles are sacred and I don't believe I am the type of person to be associated with anything sacred, except for my own prayers, though possibly also the eminations of nature. How peculiar it is, as one feels, touches or realizes his or her contact with a mystery. One is drawn like a magnet to pursue the next step and, inwardly, is pressed on to discover more, even though some vague spiritual sense may alarm one.

Harvey Howells said, "I have neither the temerity nor the learning to put down all that is known about the subject."(dowsing) All that is known about the subject would be large volumes, but evidently, all that is about to be known about the subject, are increasingly massive volumes. If men with the learning and knowledge of Harvey Howells, speak of temerity, then such men as I, with only practical knowledge and poor learning, attempting to advance the understanding of water dowsing, must be considered to have acted in a suicidal manner. It will be through the temerity (a good word) of the few, that the increasingly massive, future volumes of the knowledge of dowsing and it's possible uses in the future, will be revealed and amassed. I don' think, really, that I have acted in a suicidal manner, but I do admit to acting boldly in trying to write my first attempt, considering the lack of those assets needed for such an art form. This writing may never see the light of day, but I have enjoyed it and truly wish that many, many more people could experience and know the power of the dowsing rod.

CHAPTER 17

LAND WITHOUT WATER

I must relate an unusual occurence that took place about three months ago on the eastern slope of the Blue Ridge Mountains. I had been to the area on three occasions and marked four well sites. They were all at about the 800 foot elevation mark, with the odd rock outcropping here and there. The first well site that was drilled had the prediction of 6 gallons per minute at 160 feet depth. The first indication of water was at 150 feet, but the driller continued down to 500 feet. It was at this time that I had gone back to the property to locate another site about one quarter of a mile lower down the mountain at the farm house. The owner and I were marking the site I had located, when suddenly there was a terrific explosion higher up in the vicinity of the drilling rig. We both looked up and agreed it was up near the well being drilled and appeared to come from the drilling rig itself. We could see the operators and all seemed normal, so we went on working at marking the well location at the house, after which I left. That night I called by telephone and asked the owner if he had found out the cause of the loud explosion. He said the driller told him it was an air explosion and that he had pulled his drill out and gone to another site, as any water they had originally had had disappeared. But there were loud noises coming from the hole. I found out later that these growlings, rumblings and noises went on for two days. The owners took neighbors, workmen and friends to the site, as the noises could be heard all over the neighborhood. They did not get too close to the shaft, being afraid of what might happen. Then on the third day the noises stopped. The owner went back to the hole to check it and found that there was water within 30 feet of ground level. So they had about 470 feet of water, or 705 gallons of water in the shaft. Within 24 hours it all disappeared and the hole was dry and silent. No explanation has yet been found for this unusual occurance. My own estimation is, that the driller had punched through rock into a large cavern or chamber and when his drill went through the roof or ceiling of this underground chamber, the trapped air underground suddenly escaped up the drilled shaft, causing the explosion. Then the noises, growlings etc. were caused by the movement of air and water within the chamber, adjoining tunnels and passages. Probably some earth and rock became dislodged and blocked the water outlet, so that it filled the cavern or chamber and rose up the drilled shaft. Then the blockage must have cleared, allowing the normal flow of water underground to continue in it's original manner.

The recent sink holes of Florida are, to say the least, very unusual. But one can understand what would happen if an area that was honeycombed below ground, with the chambers full of water, gradually had that water removed, leaving the honeycombed underground dry,thus allowing pressures and stresses to work, causing cave-ins, deterioration of the honeycomb walls and an underground collapse. The rate of collapse would no doubt depend on the type of material that existed underground. Those areas that sank and were seen at the surface (sink-holes) would be minor compared to the massive collapse that might take place in the underground channels, where part of the chamber ceilings might fall in and block old passageways, leaving the surface layers thinner and weaker.

I wonder what might happen if and when the water table comes back. New channels and passageways might be formed and, due to the ceilings and upper structures having fallen down, this would mean that the new waterways underground would be closer to the surface and, in some instances, would cover certain surface areas.

We always underestimate the powers of nature and the two great destructive forces, fire and water. Each is indeed powerful, especially water, working underground and unseen where great volumes are removed and then replaced. Massive changes can take place, above and below ground.

These are just thoughts of my own and probably have no relation to the actual facts, but we are in an era of unusual circumstances, throughout the world, especially with water.

Getting back to actual dowsing again, I have had many calls recently to find well sites. It is now November 1981 and in our particular area we are in a state of drought. We have had no regular rainfall this summer and 1980 was a similar year. From the standpoint of crops etc, we have had enough rain only to suffice. The experts say, to bring the amount of rainfall to normal and bring the water table back to normal we would need 60 days of rainfall. But in the past six months, I have dowsed about fifteen well sites and nine of these have been 20 to 60 gallons per minute wells. At an average of approximately 10 gallons per minute or 600 gallons per hour, this would be in the range of 14,000 gallons per day. For single households, in actual fact, 14,000 gallons would be enough water for 140 people at 100 gallons each per day.

During this six month period I have received several letters from very happy property owners who have understood the value of abundant water and yet I have not received a " thank you for coming and helping us", from those who, though they got anywhere from 4 to 8 gallons per minute, had expected 20 to 30 gallons per minute.

I have driven miles to help people, who called by telephone, in urgent need and ask if I "could come in the morning". Some of them were prominent people of the county. I never have turned anyone down but, because of the lack of appreciation of people in general, I often feel like sayiing "I'm sorry I just can't do it any more." But I always go and help because they just do not understand and they are so helpless.

One man sent me a very nice letter. I found him 30 gallons per minute at the site of a $100,000.00 new home he was having build. He was so happy and said he could not afford to send me anything at that time, but as soon as he could he would. This is just one of very many who react in this manner; they require one's services NOW and, though they are saved $500.00 to several thousand dollars, by having a dowser find sufficient water, they are unappreciative and lack consideration. But those people who are made believers and are over-joyed with the results, make up for the bad experiences and the inconsideration of some other people.

I have recently heard that in the city of Bath, in England, where the Romans built the Great Baths from an original swamp, with engineering that astounds modern engineers, scientists have excavated below the original Roman foundations and, in the preparation of remodeling the whole complex, have found that the deep down source of the spring comes from water that is estimated to be 10,000 years old. This goes back to my previous comments; there must be massive bodies of water deep down, within the earth, that do not depend on actual rainfall for replenishment. Where we find domes of water at high points in the mountains, the water must rise from these depths, under pressure, form moving bodies within the earth, following the original paths of gases or earthquakes that raised the mountains. The deep down original source may have been bad water mixed with other chemicals, but in it's travel under pressure to the surface it passes through natural filters, and becomes purified. We know that some areas have hard lime water, some with a sulphur taste and some containing iron, depending on the layers of different sub-strata the water passed through. These are observations on my part; I have no proof, but I would wager if one picked a city of 50,000 souls and drained their present reservoirs one could drill wells and supply all the water needed.

I was a member of a commission recently, appointed by the court, to ascertain the fair value of a tract of land which was being taken by the highway department in the construction of a new road. The value of a stream on the property became an important point because of it's use for the future watering of livestock. During our debate and consideration, one member, who was born and raised in the particular area and was over sixty years of age, happened to mention a high knob-hill close by where, he said, at the highest point, a big spring broke out. It bubbled up from some rocks and gave

123

evidence of coming up through sand, as all around among the rocks, clean sand showed up through the water. It was a crystal clear spring and the water was excellent to taste and very cold on the hottest days. He went on to say that through his life he had never known this spring to go dry, even though down in the valleys there was a drought. The conversation was among men who understood the value of water. Land owners who run livestock, can have a piece of their ground taken for whatever purpose. But to take away the source of water for all the land is another question. Land without water gradually becomes useless.

Back in the pioneer days, range wars were fought over the availability of precious water and when a man settled in an area with his family and stock, his first concern was permanent water supply.

As I look out of a window here, snow is falling steadily on this 24th day of November 1981 and it is a godsend. The ground is not yet frozen, so when it does warm up and the snow melts, the water will go down into the soil, and not run off the surface as it would do if the ground was deep frozen. We have had very little snow these past few years and that which did fall came after severe frosts. So when a surface thaw came, the water ran off finally to the sea. A good blanket of snow, that would stay until springtime, was always a blessing, but we have not had the old fashioned winters we used to have. I remember back in the 1920's from the end of October the snow fell and gradually covered the fence posts three feet deep. We had no wheel traffic until March. This was in Canada of course, but the seasons have changed. The attitudes of the people have changed also. In those by gone days when the whole country depended upon agriculture, even the children in school knew the human dependency upon water. But how do you convince the computer-minded, scientifically saturated populations today, that it is very difficult to produce the water requirements of a nation in a chemical laboratory.

I noticed in the American Dowser Quarterly Digest, of November 1981 an article called WATER, by John R. McCreary. Mr. McCreary made a very interesting remark. He said three fourths of the earth is covered by water; oceans, lakes, rivers or other impoundments and he went on to ask, "Where does it all come from?" As he said, the ultimate source is God. We have been taught evaporation, clouds, rain, but there must be a very big question there.

I go back in this writing to my thoughts of the great deserts and I repeat, "The many oases in the Sahara, 50 to 200 miles apart, with their clumps of date palms, have been there for thousands of years and have been used by thousands of camel trains. These watering holes along the great trails, treated with reverence by the Arabs and the nations of traders of those days, are still, today, the only sources of water in this gigantic world of sand. Rain is sparse in the Sahara, but if it rained heavily for days, the first few feet of sand would absorb the rain and within hours after the downpour all would be parched dry again." Where, then, does the supply of water come from that has kept these oasis water holes supplied for many thousands of years?

There must be enormous pressures moving within the Earth and, under such pressures, liquids find their way to the surface at the points of least resistance. When oil is found at great depths, it comes forth first under great pressure. When water is found, it generally rises within the shaft or casing, from far below ground level, and then maintains it's level for many years, or until movements or pressures are altered deep below the surface.

I remember one well site I found at a depth of several hundred feet. It came in at 130 gallons per minute and ran over continually until a pump was put on it and it was sealed off.

Evidence upon evidence becomes peculiarly strong, pointing to the existance of permanent massive bodies of water, flowing within the Earth.

Again I am by no means competant to follow through on these thoughts or observations, but I believe the eventual lack of good water will bring about a complete change in the attitudes of many around the world.

For you who may read this, persue the thought and ask questions, water is our life's blood and without it all life must perish.

"PARTIAL LIST OF WELL SITES DOWSED"

The following are those well sites, locations and names of owners here within Loudoun County, Common-Wealth of Virginia of which I have kept a rough record. They are sites that can be easily located and seen. There are 60 in all.

Marcus, Rt.691, Lovettesville
  House and nursery site   140 ft. 10 g.p.m.
New house, near Dutchman's Creek
  Residential   200 ft. 16 g.p.m.
Col. Johnston, Taylorstown
  New log home   220 ft. 25 g.p.m.
Rumsfelt, Rt. 690, Hillsboro
  Future new home (not drilled yet)
Pisan, Rt. 658, North of Luckett's
  (2 sites) Satisfactory
Carlton, Hillsboro
  New construction begun   300 ft. 9 g.p.m.
Ottinger, Hillsboro
  New home   180 ft. 25 g.p.m.
Stupar, Hillsboro, Tenant house
  Spring gone dry   150 ft. 20 g.p.m.
Stupar, Hillsboro Farm house
  Needed more water   120 ft. 6 g.p.m.
Altizer, Sunny Ridge
  North of Round Hill   300 ft. 4 g.p.m.
Bird, Sunny Ridge, Spring gone dry
  Half acre and Cottage   120 ft. 7 g.p.m.
Town of Round Hill, 2 sites
  Not used--Prediction   40 & 60 g.p.m.
Hoyle, Round Hill
  3 sites (new homes)   93 ft. 20 g.p.m.
                                  107 ft. 13 g.p.m.
                                  67 ft. 4 g.p.m.

Mainhart, Round Hill
  3 sites (not yet drilled)
McDaniel, The Trapp, Rt. 626
  Old home   170 ft. 18 g.p.m.
Tyler, Bloomfield, Spring failed
  Old farm   150 ft. 10 g.p.m.

Mayo-Brown, Middleburg	
Farm	280 ft. 8 g.p.m.
Old Quaker House, Waterford	
Spring gone	65 ft. 40 g.p.m.
Insurance Company, Waterford	
Very poor area	300 ft. 2 g.p.m.
Gore, Rt. 738, Hamilton	
New home	180 ft. 7 g.p.m.
Gore, Rt. 738, Hamilton	
New home	200 ft. 10 g.p.m.
Gore, Rt. 738	
Farm	220 ft. 16 g.p.m.
Raymand, Hamilton	
New home	200 ft. 20 g.p.m.
Bradshaw, Hamilton, 200 acre	
Housing project (3 sites)	
(Wells used to supply water for	
whole project)	30,40 & 60 g.p.m.
Brown, Rt. 709, Hamilton	
Dairy farm	140 ft. 16 g.p.m.
Smallwood, Rt. 722, Lincoln	
New home	200 ft. 25 g.p.m.
Maxwell, Mt. Gilead	
New home	165 ft. 25 g.p.m.
Burkbile, Mt. Gilead, Poluted well	
(Map dowsed first)	240 ft. 15 g.p.m.
Cabin, Rt. 631	
Mountain Road	175 ft. 20 g.p.m.
Cross, Rt. 772, Arcola	
New home	160 ft. 12 g.p.m.
O'Brien, Rt. 9, Peaonians Springs	
New home	170 ft. 8 g.p.m.
Animal Shelter, Waterford	
(4 sites) All excellent	
(They now have large pond)	
Harrison, Rt. 704, Dairy farm	
New house	160 ft. 25 g.p.m.
Cross, Rt. 769, Old Colonial home	
(Being remodeled)	165 ft.100 g.p.m.
Town of Leesburg, (8 sites) checked	
and predicted, but engineers felt the	
dowsing approach was not scientific	

Judge-Penn, Rt. 15, North		
New home	125 ft.	25 g.p.m.
Lucier, Rt. 15, North		
New home	150 ft.	100 g.p.m.
Lucas Phillips, Rt 7, West		
(never drilled) Fort Johnston	160 ft.	8 g.p.m.
Penn, Rt. 7, West		
Fort Johnston	300 ft.	3 g.p.m.
Warner, Rt. 7, West		
New Home, Fort Johnston	280 ft.	3 g.p.m.
Va-Iden Zieler, (Rock-Knob)		
New home	200 ft.	2 g.p.m.
Wright-Leesburgh Golf Course	165 ft.	60 g.p.m.
Wright Golf Course		
Garden Apts.	180 ft.	125 g.p.m.
Lyman, Leesburg (50 acres) 140 homes		
(3 sites)	all at	40 g.p.m.
National Children's Rehabilitation Center		
(3 sites) Map dowsed. To be drilled		
Jewel, Rt. 15, South		
New home	160 ft.	100 g.p.m.
Granada, Rt. 621, Farm		
(Water for livestock)	180 ft.	100 g.p.m.
Urban-Church, Rt. 621	200 ft.	25 g.p.m.
Rolling Acres, Subdivision, New homes		
(10 sites) Average	130 ft.	20 g.p.m.
. Blunt, Rt. 650, South		
New home	188 ft.	28 g.p.m.
Jewel, Rt. 704, South		
New home	150 ft.	8 g.p.m.
Bortman, Chantilly		
Stone quarry	380 ft.	22 g.p.m.
Borah, Chantilly		
3 New homes average		15 g.p.m.
Owen, Near Chantilly, New home		
(Had drilled 2 wells)	165 ft.	6 g.p.m.
Hollsinger, Rt. 704, South		
& Rt. 797, New home	180 ft.	12 g.p.m.
Leesburg Motors, Rt. 7, East	300 ft.	4 g.p.m.

POSTSCRIPT

In going over a partial list of wells which I have dowsed, I came up with some very interesting figures for 60 of the well sites:

Average depth	141 feet
Average flow	25 g.p.m.
Total depth	8,477 ft.
Total flow	1,550 g.p.m.
Total daily flow	2,232,000 gal.
Total flow, per day, per site	37,200 gal.

The standard requirement is 100 gallons of water, per person per day.

The town of Leesburg uses for all purposes 1,800,000 gallons per day for a population of approximately 8,000, plus all other uses. This is approximately 225 gallons per person per day. (The cost is metered per gallons per household).

If you take the total flow of 60 well sites, 2,232,000 gallons per day, and say the average maximum is 10 persons per well site, this then comes out at 60 well sites x 10 people or 600 people. Divide this into 2,232,000 gallons=3,720 gallons per person per day, of good pure deep well water. Except for the initial cost of well, pump etc, this is cheap water, with no chemicals added, generally.

I do not know how many private wells there are in the county, but this average of 60 wells is a good guide to the average of depth and flow in the county; also to the enormous quantity of underground water available, which is very seldom affected by drought and has little dependency on rainfall, as is the case with reservoirs and impoundments. I felt the foregoing facts and figures were of considerable interest and may prove to be of much greater significant value in the future. I read that some of the northeastern states were having trouble with arsenic in certain well sites. This condition was spread over a wide area, which again suggests that water travels underground, in streams of quantity, and for some considerable distance.

This immediately conjures up thoughts of land fill dumps, chemical dumps, septic systems and interference with nature's underground supply of good potable water.

The source of a river is generally a trickle of crystal clear water from under a rock high in the hill country. It comes forth clean and sweet and very soon becomes victim to thoughtless humans, who turn it into poison before it reaches the sea.

ADDITIONAL READING

HENRY GROSS AND HIS DOWSING ROD
by Kenneth Roberts
Doubleday & Company, Inc.

DOWSING FOR EVERYONE
by Harvey Howells
The Stephen Greene Press
Brattleboro, Vermont

WATER UNLIMITED
by Kenneth Roberts
Doubleday & Company, Inc.

THE DIVINING HAND
By Christopher Bird
E. P. Dutton, New York

MODERN DOWSING
by Raymond C. Willey
Esoteric Publications
Phoenix, Arizona

AQUAVIDEO
by Verne L. Cameron
El Cariso Publications
Santa Barbara, California

PRACTICAL DOWSING
by Robert T. McKusick
The Association of Universal Philosophy
Globe, Arizona

A FIELD GUIDE TO DOWSING
By Gordon MacLean
The American Society of Dowsers, Inc.
Danville, Vermont

STEPS TO DOWSING POWER
By Bruce and Shirley Wayland
Life Force Press
Phoenix, Arizona

INDEX

Africa, 64
Africa, British Government in, 18
Alexander, Cecil Frances, 3
Altizer, 27
American Continent, 73
American Dowser, The, 88, 97
American Dowser Quarterly Digest, 124
American Society of Dowsers, 76, 103
Animal Shelter, 28
Aquifer, 97, 104
Arctic Circle, 72
Atlantic Ocean, 73, 74

Barnes, Gordon, 35, 96, 97
Bermuda, 13, 35, 97, 111
Big Springs, 91, 114
Biolocational, 93, 104
Biophysical, 93, 104
Bird, 127
Bishops Rule, 17, 85
Black Jack Area, 30
Blue Ridge Mountains, 12, 29, 66, 88, 95, 98, 120
Blunt, Joe, 36, 129
Borah, 129
Border Country, 81, 95, 99
Bortman, Arnold, 57, 129
Bradley, Bill, 87, 97
Bradshaw, 128
Branson, Ethel, 1
Branson, Oscar, 1
British Columbia, 18
British Dowsing Association, 103
British Government, 18
British Isles, 81, 104
British Society of Dowsers, 76
Brookfield Farm, 42
Brown, 128
Bull Run, 12
Burkbile, 128

Canada, 10, 73, 124

Hatcher, Tom, 5, 6, 12, 13, 21, 52, 85, 86, 90, 92, 97, 112, 113, 114
Health Department, 19, 22, 100
Heilman, Colonel, 25
Hereford Journal, 10
Holden, Peter Randolph, 48
Hollsinger, 129
Howells, Harvey, 6, 25, 26, 33, 76, 94, 95, 98, 117, 119
Hoyle, I.L., 39, 127
Hudson River, 30, 76
Hydrogeology, 88

Jewel, Don, 84, 85, 129
Jewel, Mr., 84, 129
Johnston, Colonel, 127
Judge-Penn, 129

Kakaroff, Bruce, 69
King, Les, 14
Kuralt, Charles, 96

"Lang May Yer'r Lum Reek", 5, 80
Lawson, Harry "Buck", 28, 29, 40, 45, 85
Leesburg Golf & Country Club, 27, 38
Leesburg Motors, 129
Lehmann, Robert O., 38
Lind, Robert, 109, 113
Lindsay, Francis, 37
Lindsay, Judy, 37
Loudoun County, 10, 14, 66, 95, 109, 111, 112, 114
Lucier, James, 84, 129
Lyman, 53-54, 129

Magna Group Inc., 38
Maine, 113
Maine, Kennebunkport, 112
Mainhart, 127
Map Dowsing, 22-23, 32-33, 53, 81-82, 90, 93, 98, 100
Marcus, 127
Maryland, 12, 33, 86
Maryland, Hagerstown, 52
Mason, Colonel, 12, 13, 111, 112

Pliers, dowsing with, 71, 72, 111
Poor Richards Almanac, 104
Potomac River, 12, 13, 20, 76, 86, 97

R.A.F., 10, 14, 64, 69
Raymand, 128
Richards, Barbara, 34, 68, 73, 118
Roberts, Kenneth, 6, 12, 14, 26, 64, 69, 111, 113
Rolling Acres, Subdivision, 129
Ross, Terry, 8, 76
Rumsfelt, 127

Sahara Desert, 34, 97, 125
Scotland, 80, 81, 95
Second World War, 10, 73
Short Hill, The, 12
Smallwood, 128
Smithett, P.B., 76
Snyder, Woody, 47
Soviet Union, 104
St.Lawrence River, 76
Stupar, 127
Subterranean movements, 34

Taylor, Elwin, 76
Texas, 70
Trapp, The, 127
Tri County Construction Company, 40
Tuscarora Creek, 27, 28
Tyler, Jim, 66, 67, 68, 127

U.S.A., 4, 10, 33, 81, 104
U.S.S.R., 93
U.S.S.R., Ministry of Geology, 93
Urban-Church, 129

Varty, John, 11, 12
Virginia, 12, 20, 63, 66, 76
Virginia;
    Arcola, 128
    Bloomfield, 127
    Chantilly, 129
    Dutchman's Creek, 127

"Isn't it amazing what a Y Branch
from a tree can lead to?"

Water
Divining
Service

"Dick" A. Richards
Box 367
Leesburg
Va. 22075